MENTAL HEALTH
Awareness

MENTAL HEALTH
Awareness
BLACK & BROWN PAIN

LAQUITA D. WRIGHT

Copyright © 2020 by Laquita D. Wright.

Library of Congress Control Number:		2020919462
ISBN:	Hardcover	978-1-6641-2559-9
	Softcover	978-1-6641-2557-5
	eBook	978-1-6641-2558-2

All rights reserved. No part of this book may be reproduced or transmitted in any form or by any means, electronic or mechanical, including photocopying, recording, or by any information storage and retrieval system, without permission in writing from the copyright owner.

Any people depicted in stock imagery provided by Getty Images are models, and such images are being used for illustrative purposes only.
Certain stock imagery © Getty Images.

Print information available on the last page.

Rev. date: 10/09/2020

To order additional copies of this book, contact:
Xlibris
844-714-8691
www.Xlibris.com
Orders@Xlibris.com
815407

CONTENTS

Summary xv
Introduction xvii

Chapter 1   Origin 1
    Post Traumatic Slave Syndrome (PTSS) 1

Chapter 2   Facts of Life: The Stigma of Mental Illness in
               Black and Brown Communities 11

Chapter 3   Medical System/Historical Abuse in Black and
               Brown Communities 15

    Medical System 15
    Historical Abuse 16
    In Modern Times 17

Chapter 4   Faith and Spirituality versus Mental Health
               Care in Black and Brown Communities 20

    Misconceptions about Mental Illness 21

Chapter 5   Mental Health Advocate: Taraji P. Henson 24

    Celebrity Talk 25

Chapter 6   Homicidal versus Suicidal: The White versus
               Black Youth in Black and Brown Communities 28

    Jail versus Mental Institution in Black and Brown
        Communities 34
    21 Harsh Truths Black People Don't Want to Hear 40

Chapter 7   Research on Inequality in the Health Care System ... 43

    Coverage Gains—and Obstacles—for African
        Americans Under the ACA 44
    The South's Stubborn Approach to Medicaid Expansion ... 45
    Disparities in Health Outcomes 47
    Important Considerations for Health Care Specific to
        African Americans 49
    Racism's Wear and Tear on African Americans 49
    Poverty 51
    Household Income Inequality 51
    The Wealth Gap 52
    Food Insecurity 52
    Medicare for All 55
    Public Insurance Option 55
    Ensuring Health Care Access and Affordable
        Coverage for African Americans 57
    Promote health equity by adequately addressing 58
    Chapter 7 References 60

Chapter 8   Types of Depression 66

    Depression 66

Chapter 9   Black, Asian and Minority Ethnic (BAME)
                Communities 74

    Racism and discrimination 74
    Social and economic inequalities 74
    Criminal justice system 75
    Other factors 76
    Mental health stigma 76
    Different BAME groups and particular mental health
        concerns 76
    Asian/ Asian British 77
    Further Information and Resources 79

Chapter 10 Policing AmeriKKK in Black and Brown
            Communities 80

Chapter 11 When Racism Takes Over Health Care in Black
            and Brown Communities 84

    Racism Is a Mental Illness in Black and Brown
            Communities 85

Index 99

To my beautiful daughter who inspired me to write this book because she wants to become an author one day. Watching and sharing life with my daughter, Quanayia, has taught me more than I ever dreamed possible. This book is also respectfully dedicated to my beloved mother, my grandmother, uncle, and granddad. May they rest in peace, these beautiful queens and kings who taught me everything I know in so little time. Thank you. Lastly, dedicating this book to the world and my ancestors, hoping this book changes the generational curses and help heal hearts, minds, and souls.

You can't fix what you don't understand, so you have to understand in order to know where you can heal.
—Laquita D. Wright

You don't know where you are going until you know where you been.
—Karen D. Wright

Help Us Too!

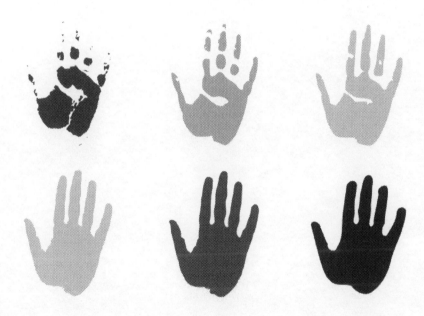

Summary

This book boldly confronts the reality of black and brown mental pain head on. There is a systematic and racist belief that black/brown people can deal with and ignore pain better than any other race. Speaking from experience in the minority communities of America, there is a negative stigma surrounding mental health. Instead of seeking professional help for conditions, such as PTSD, depression, and anxiety, many resort to self-medication, drug, opioids, alcohol, etc., or isolation in an attempt to solve their problem on their own. Black/brown people are reluctant to discuss mental health issues and seek treatment because of the shame and stigma still associated with such conditions in our communities. As a black person, it is not easy to express emotional pain because we are told not to show those emotions. I am approaching it both from community education and cultural competency perspective.

I know that black and brown people are hurting. I know because I am one of them. *Mental Health Awareness: Black and Brown Pain* sheds light on the need to improve access to mental health treatment within the underrepresented communities. For many centuries, the indigenous people of color have experienced trauma in all aspects of their lives. This book is a must-read and a guide to finding relief through mental help.

Introduction

Growing up, I felt shameful talking about my depression. Certain family members would tell me I do not need help or antidepressants because black people do not take medication or talk to a therapist for mental illness. A large percentage of the minority communities do not believe in seeing a therapist. There's nothing but faith and Jesus. We are told to go to church and pray about it. Since I was a little girl, I was called crazy, a cry baby, shy, quiet, and everybody around me kept saying I have an attitude problem. My loved ones did not understand the entire time, calling me names. I was silently suffering from depression all alone. Black families rarely talk about feelings, so it is so hard to express them without someone passing judgment, which is a typical Christian move. My mother was unaware of my mental illness because she had no knowledge of what mental health care was. The only thing my mother knew was I became angry and violent over time. I was keeping traumatizing secrets away from my mother because I felt like no one would believe me. Depression is not an attitude problem; it is a character weakness. Crying spells are a sign of depression, and being quiet is a sign of abuse. As an adult, I realize how unaware black families were about mental health care. This book is personal and dear to my heart as a woman of color. I see the world differently, and writing this self-help book will bring great awareness, letting the world know that my mind is still suffering from mental illness every day. I am finally aware of how I can heal myself and other black and brown people.

Since I was seven, I felt depressed. It took me till I turned twenty-five to acknowledge my depression and childhood trauma on my own. Now in my midthirties, I want to finally bring awareness. Never getting the opportunity to speak about it broke me down mentally, emotionally, and physically in the past decade. Being black or brown in "AmeriKKK" is a constant mental pain and challenge. Understanding the damage society has caused people of color mentally; even our own families cause mental pain. We, as minorities, suffer on a daily basis in so many ways. It causes psychological distress in our communities more than any other race.

This book will bring awareness to everyone all over the world in regard to mental health in minority communities. The fear of telling people I needed help cause me to go through mental illness on my own. God has a big influence as to why I am writing this book about black and brown pain. The black and brown community suffers from an increased rate of mental health concerns. I want to bring this to everyone's attention. What you think you may know about minorities and mental health may be wrong! Unfortunately, many Europeans have a hard time even hearing a person of color express their feelings and experiences about mental health. We do not have access to mental health care like other races due to socioeconomic and racial disparities, such as the exclusion from health, education, social, and economic resources. Black and brown people are born with depression. Trauma affects the DNA; it is in our blood vessels. Multigenerational maladaptive behavior, also known as PTSS, which originates as survival strategies for minorities. Four hundred plus years of trauma/slavery cause post-traumatic slavery syndrome, which has not caught the attention of many Americans, including black and brown people. We are born with depression that no other race goes through. Through the centuries, our ancestors were beaten and mentally enslaved. Enslaved women went through pain, carrying stress in her body that will genetically become stressful on babies who are not even born yet. We are still suffering from past pain, and our mental Illness is more disabling and takes a greater toll on all aspects of our lives, including work, relationships, and social concern.

As a young teenager, I grew up surrounded by violence and abuse. If you were to ask me, black-on-black crime will be the death of our race, not just police brutality and the justice system. Everyone I knew was angry and sad, making bad decisions as kids and adults due to poverty, trauma, and not having a way out. Some of us were traumatized as children who live without parents. Never letting go of childhood trauma causes us to become emotionally disturbed inside. What happens when we are left undiagnosed and untreated for mental health? You either become suicidal or have homicidal thoughts! Are we criminals? or are we mentally ill? Do we need jail time or a mental institution? There is a deep stigma against mental illness and health care in the black and brown communities. We are dealing with the corrupt justice system, mass incarceration, structural racism, and socioeconomic racial disparities. We are also dealing with self-hate and hatred with one another. It practically became normal to see violence and abuse in the projects of America. We, as colored people, think it's okay and it's fun to watch someone being harmed. To me, that is a mental illness that needs to be addressed. The situation is fueled by prejudices, misunderstandings, misconceptions, and sometimes, racism that creates a circle of fear and a lack of trust in the medical system due to historical abuse, which leads to poor treatment. We need a clear explanation for our troubles and a guide to finding relief through building a supportive network and access to medical health care for black and brown pain.

We feel in our mind something is wrong, but we do not know what it is. I do not think people realize how much strength it takes to pull your own self out of a dark place mentally with no help because no one believes in mental health. So if you have done that alone today or any day, I am proud of you.

This book's aim is to provide contextual focus and awareness on the position of black and brown mental health issues in America. It is an attempt to encourage Europeans and minorities to break the silence by bringing awareness to the black and brown communities.

1

Origin

Post Traumatic Slave Syndrome (PTSS)

PTTS is described as a set of behaviors and actions associated with or related to multigenerational trauma experienced by black and brown people but is not limited to undiagnosed or untreated PTSD in enslaved Africans and their descendants. PTSD is a mental condition that results in a series of emotional and physical reactions in individuals who have either witnessed or experienced traumatic events. PTTS maladaptive behavior cannot be cured clinically like PTSD but must be repaired by a profound structural change in society. Maladaptive behavior originates as survival strategies passed down for generations. PTTS arose after many ex-slaves' experienced socially dysfunctional relationships and struggled with self-destructive impulses for centuries. The experience did not fade over time but continued through generations, genetically speaking. Trauma is in the DNA of all descendants of ex-slaves. Those who descended from ex-slave ancestors will have a chance of suffering from PTSS and PTSD in their lifetime. Is there support to the theory of PTSS in terms of the black and brown communities? Yes. Researcher, Dr. Joy DeGruy, developed her theory of PTSS in 2005. She thinks that actual past memories are being transmitted through our DNA, which is an indirect traumatic experience. Living in black and brown skin is a whole different level of stress. The four hundred years of slavery was abolished, but trauma continued to be deeply rooted in the blood vessels of black and brown people who suffered from multigenerational oppression. Past pain comes from centuries of slavery. There is a big misperception of American behavior toward minorities. PTSS eventually turns into PTSD over time due to stress that has been inherited from the bodies of our ancestors. Have you ever gotten mad for no reason out the blue? Happy one minute and, seconds later, become angry? Every black and brown person in AmeriKKK experienced it before or will in their lifetime! The chains in our DNA is real! During slavery, our descendants were dehumanized and used as free labor and for domestic work and sexual advantages. Slave masters raped and molested both men and women during slavery. Emotionally disturbed, easily influenced, abused, and traumatized cause generations to suffer mentally. Slaves were tricked into working against each other a method called "Willie Lynch," named after a slave owner. Now you hear black on brown crime is at an all-time high in AmeriKKK today, and the method has been working for centuries. We will always be mentally enslaved if we do not create a structural change in minority communities. Every race experiences PTSD recently, but black and brown people are experiencing both past and present trauma. The descendants of the ex-slaves feel their ancestors' spirits and put them in an emotional state, thinking about past events, which make us have anxiety, anger, depression, homicidal thoughts, PTTS, and PTSD.

White Americans have failed to indicate any remorse for the actions taken against black and brown people and how much it affects our DNA and the generations to come. PTSS posits that centuries of slavery in the United States, followed by systemic and structural racism and oppression, including lynching, Jim Crow laws, and unwarranted mass incarceration have resulted in multigenerational maladaptive behaviors, which originated as survival strategies. The syndrome continues because children, whose parents suffer from PTSS, are often indoctrinated into the same behaviors long after the behaviors have lost their contextual effectiveness. DeGruy states that PTSS is not a disorder that can simply be treated and remedied clinically but, rather, also requires a profound social change in individuals, as well as in institutions that continue to reify inequality and injustice toward the descendants of enslaved Africans.

Post Traumatic Slave Syndrome: America's Legacy of Enduring Injury and Healing (PTSS) is a 2005 theoretical work by Joy DeGruy.

Breaking News, June 18, 2020

Update: Lloyd's of London Apologizes for Its 'Shameful' Role in Atlantic Slave Trade
Guy Faulconbridge, Kaye Holton, *Insurance Journal*, June 18, 2020, https://www.insurancejournal.com/news/international/2020/06/18/572696.htm

A day before June eighteenth, the Lloyd's of London insurance market has apologized for its "shameful" role in the 18th and 19th Century Atlantic slave trade and pledged to fund opportunities for black and ethnic minority groups. About 17 million African men, women and children were torn from their homes and shackled into one of the world's most brutal globalized trades between the 15th and 19th centuries. Many died in merciless conditions. "We are sorry for the role played by the Lloyd's market in the 18th and 19th Century slave trade—an appalling and shameful period of English history, as well as our own," Lloyd's said in a statement on Thursday. "Recent events have shone a spotlight on the inequality that black people have experienced over many years as a result of systematic and structural racism that has existed in many aspects of society and unleashed difficult conversations that were long overdue," it added. The world's leading commercial insurance market, Lloyd's—which started life in Edward Lloyd's coffee house in 1688—is where complex insurance contracts ranging from catastrophe to events cancellation are agreed and underwritten. Lloyd's grew to dominate the shipping insurance market, a key element of Europe's global scramble for empire, treasure and slaves, who were usually in the 18th century included in insurance policies in the general rate for ship cargo. Weapons and gunpowder from Europe were swapped for African slaves who were shipped across the Atlantic to the Americas. Those who survived endured a life of subjugation on plantations, while the ships returned to Europe laden with sugar, cotton, and tobacco. Although Britain abolished the trans-Atlantic slave trade in 1807, full abolition did not follow for another generation. Lloyd's said it would invest in programs to attract black and minority ethnic talent, review its artifacts to ensure they were not racist and support charities and organizations promoting opportunity for black and minority ethnic people. 'Inexcusable' A sweeping global reassessment of history and racism has been triggered by the May 25 death of George Floyd, a black man who died after a Minneapolis police officer knelt on his neck for nearly nine minutes while detaining him. An Oxford University college said on Wednesday it wanted to remove a statue of 19th century colonialist Cecil Rhodes that has been a target of anti-racism protests. And Greene King, which describes itself as Britain's leading pub owner and brewer, apologized for the profit one of its original founders made from the slave trade. "It is inexcusable that one of our founders profited from slavery and argued against its abolition in the 1800s," Green King's chief executive Nick Mackenzie said. Green King would make investments to help the black, Asian and minority ethnic (BAME) community and to support race diversity in its business, Mackenzie added. The history of several other British financial firms, including Barclays is also under fresh scrutiny. The bank was named after David Barclay, a Quaker who campaigned actively against slavery in the late 18th century, but it later acquired institutions with links to the slave trade, including Colonial Bank in 1918 and Martins Bank in 1969. "We can't change what's gone before us, only how we go forward," a Barclays spokesman said. "We are committed as a bank to do more to further foster our culture of inclusiveness, equality and diversity, for our colleagues, and the customers and clients we serve." The City of London Corporation has launched the Tackling Racism Working Party, which it said will look to promote economic, educational, and social inclusion in the City of London and assess the future of statues and monuments. (Writing by Guy Faulconbridge; additional reporting by Sinead Cruise and Huw Jones; editing by William Schomberg, Edmund Blair, and Alexander Smith)

Question: As a descendant of an ex-slave how Lloyd of London and Green King will repay every black person who the bloodline of those are who were enslaved over 400 years?

"Ethnicity," Future Culture at Lloyd's, https://futurecultureat.lloyds.com/culture-update/ethnicity/

Lloyd of London's Answer

At Lloyd's we understand that we cannot always be proud of our past. In particular, we are sorry for the role played by the Lloyd's market in the eighteenth and nineteenth century slave trade—an appalling and shameful period of English history, as well as our own. In acknowledging our own history, we also remain committed to focusing on the actions we can take today to shape our future into one that we can truly be proud to stand by.

Over the last week, we have listened carefully to our Black and Ethnic Minority colleagues in the Lloyd's market. We have heard their frustrations, and it is clear that we must commit now as a market to take meaningful and measurable action.

Building an inclusive culture is essential to the market's future success and that is why culture sits alongside performance and strategy as one of the Corporation's three strategic priorities.

And we are not alone—through initiatives like Inclusion@Lloyd's and Dive In, the wider Lloyd's market has in recent years thrown its collective resources behind the drive for greater diversity and inclusion across the piece. We have made progress, but not enough.

Therefore, today we are announcing a number of initiatives to help improve the experience of Black and Minority Ethnic talent in the Lloyd's market We will:

1. Invest in positive programs to attract, retain and develop Black and Minority Ethnic talent in the Lloyd's market,

including launching our 'Accelerate' Program – a modular program to develop Ethnic Minority Future Leaders across the market.

2. Review our employee and partner policies, as well as our organizational artefacts, to ensure that they are explicitly non-racist.

3. Commit to education and research. We will educate our colleagues and continue our research into the experiences of Black and Ethnic Minority professionals working in insurance, and share what we learn with the market.

4. Provide financial support to charities and organizations promoting opportunity and inclusion for Black and Ethnic minority groups.

5. Develop a long-term action plan in collaboration with our Culture Advisory Group, Black and Minority Ethnic colleagues and white allies who will inform our journey and hold us to account. We are grateful to our Black and Ethnic Minority colleagues who have helped to shape our conversations and actions to ensure that we create an environment free from injustice for them and for all. Our commitment is that we will continue to listen and learn as we act and to measure our progress.

There is a long way to go but we are determined that we can and will create a culture in the Lloyd's market in which everybody can flourish.

Recent events have shone a spotlight on the inequality that black people have experienced over many years as a result of systematic and structural racism that has existed in many aspects of society and unleashed difficult conversations that were long overdue.

In the biggest deportation in known history, weapons and gunpowder from Europe were swapped for millions of African slaves, who were then shipped across the Atlantic to the Americas. Ships returned to Europe with sugar, cotton, and tobacco. Around 17 million African men, women and children were torn from their homes and shackled into one of the world's most brutal globalized trades between the 15th and 19th centuries. Many died in merciless conditions. As a descendant and as a Black American we deserve more than any handout from a company who believes in slavery, selling human beings for centuries. Black American deserves reparations from every company who were involved in selling my ancestors and profiting off of them. We as Black Americans deserve more, and we will fight until there is no more fight left in us as a people.

Lloyd's of London apologises over founders' slavery ties
Mia Wallace, Insurance Business UK, insurancebusinessmag. com, June 18, 2020, https://www.insurancebusinessmag. com/asia/news/breaking-news/lloyds-of-london- apologises-over-founders-slavery-ties-225613.aspx

As reported by *The Telegraph*, Lloyd's of London has pledged to pay compensation to black, Asian and minority ethnic (BAME) communities after its role in the slave trade was highlighted in an academic database. The database revealed that Simon Frasier, a founder subscriber member of Lloyd's was paid almost £400,000 (adjusted for today's currency) to surrender an estate in Dominica. Alongside the pub chain Greene King, Lloyd's has apologized for the role it historically played in the slave trade and has promised to provide financial support to charities and organizations promoting opportunity and inclusion for BAME ethnic groups. These payments mark the first time that the controversy over the UK's past involvement with slavery has impacted the corporate sector. A Lloyd's spokesman told *The Telegraph*: "We are sorry for the role played by the Lloyd's market in the 18th and 19th-century slave trade. This was an appalling and shameful period of English history, as well as our own, and we condemn the indefensible wrongdoing that occurred during this period." Speaking with the BBC, Dr. Katie Donninton, a senior lecturer in history at the London South Bank University noted that it is an important step for firms with historical links to trans-Atlantic slavery to begin the process of acknowledging the past. She welcomed the commitment by Lloyd's but said the offer of investment in BAME charities and organizations must be scrutinized to discern how much will be invested and who will receive the money.

"This is a history which is specific to the black community," she said, "and directing forms of reparative justice towards descendent groups must be the priority."

The pub chain and brewer Greene King and the insurance market Lloyd's of London both revealed on Wednesday evening that they would be making the reparations.

The news, first reported by the Telegraph, comes as people outraged by the killing of an African American man in Minnesota, George Floyd, as well as continuing racial discrimination closer to home, demand that the UK recognize the ongoing legacy of the British empire's extensive role in the enslavement of millions of Africans. Records archived by researchers at University College London (UCL) show that one of Greene King's founders, Benjamin Greene, held at least 231 human beings in slavery and became an enthusiastic supporter of the practice. When slavery was abolished in the British empire in 1833, the government agreed to pay compensation, not to the enslaved people, but to the slaveholders. The records show Greene was given the equivalent of about £500,000 at today's rate when he surrendered rights to plantations in Montserrat and Saint Kitts. He handed over control of his brewery to his son three years later and it was given its current name after a merger in 1887. Several of Greene's descendants went on to hold prominent positions in British society, including a Bank of England governor, Conservative MP, and BBC director general. "It is inexcusable that one of our founders profited from slavery and argued against its abolition in the 1800s," said Nick Mackenzie, Greene King's chief executive officer on Wednesday. "We don't have all the answers, so that is why we are taking time to listen and learn from all the voices, including our team members and charity partners as we strengthen our diversity and inclusion work." Mackenzie added that the firm will "make a substantial investment to benefit the BAME community and support our race diversity in the business". He added that the firm now employs people "across the UK from all backgrounds", adding that "racism and discrimination have no place at Greene King". Lloyd's of London said it would "invest in positive programs to attract, retain and develop black and minority ethnic talent", as well as providing "financial support to charities and organizations promoting opportunity and inclusion for black and minority ethnic groups". A spokesman said Lloyd's was in the process of identifying suitable groups, while Greene King is understood to be consulting on which would be most appropriate. Neither firm was able to say on Wednesday evening how much money they intended to pay in charitable donations or investments in relevant schemes. The UCL records show that Simon Fraser, a founder subscriber member of Lloyd's, held at least 162 people in slavery and was paid the equivalent of nearly £400,000 at today's rate for ceding a plantation in Dominica, while yet more were held at a site in British Guiana researchers believe either belonged to him or to his son. "Lloyd's has a long and rich history dating back over 330 years, but there are some aspects of our history that we are not proud of. In particular, we are sorry for the role played by the Lloyd's market in the eighteenth and nineteenth century slave trade. This was an appalling and shameful period of English history, as well as our own, and we condemn the indefensible wrongdoing that occurred during this period," a spokesman said on Wednesday.

The firm said it wanted to both acknowledge its history and identify what it could do to foster a more inclusive culture in the present. Besides the investments, it said it intended to provide education and research, as well as reviewing its "organizational artefacts to ensure that they are explicitly non-racist". The spokesman added: "We are grateful to our black and minority ethnic colleagues who have helped to shape our conversations and actions to ensure that we create an environment free from injustice for them and for all. Our commitment is that we will continue to listen and learn as we act and to measure our progress. "There is a long way to go but we are determined that we can and will create a culture in the Lloyd's market in which everybody can flourish." Records show that, far from a system involving a few wealthy slaveholders, many ordinary Britons benefited directly from fairly small stakes in the trans-Atlantic slave trade, while the country in general grew rich as a result of its proceeds.

2

Facts of Life: The Stigma of Mental Illness in Black and Brown Communities

Black and brown grandmothers and mothers always told us to suppress: "Just be quiet, chalk it up, get up, get dress, fix your face, put on your best outfit, and just keep going." During slavery, they were supposed to be the strong ones or their master would beat or rape them. They were supposed to just do and not speak, said Esney M. Sharpe, founder and CEO of the Bessie Mae Women's Health Center in East Orange, New Jersey, which offers health and services for uninsured and underserved women. She said that cultural habits and historical experiences can cause depression to be expressed and addressed differently among black and brown people. Since 1949, the month of May has been recognized as Mental Health Month. With African Americans leading the country with troubling statistics in areas like unemployment, child abuse, and neglect, and domestic violence, all of which can exacerbate stress, it is perhaps not surprising that the African American community leads the country in mental health struggles. There is no getting around it; institutional racism is a leading cause of mental illness in African Americans. In the early 1970s, the final report of the Joint Commission on Mental Health of Children acknowledged that racism was, for some, America's "number one public health problem." Granted, it is not the only cause, but racism can psychologically affect blacks by allowing society to deny their value as individuals and by compelling them to internalize the racist conceptions of themselves. Racist stressors may also lead to increased physiological reactivity, which, when sustained for a period of time, can lead to cardiovascular disorders and diseases. For African American adults, perceived racism may cause mental health symptoms similar to trauma and could lead to some physical health disparities between blacks and other populations in the United States, according to a study published by the American

Psychological Association. Most Americans, particularly African Americans, underestimate the impact of mental disorders. Many believe symptoms of mental illnesses, such as depression, are "just the blues." Often, African Americans turn to family, church, and the community to cope. Forgiveness and grace are, indeed, hallmarks of the black church. In one study, approximately 85 percent of African Americans respondents described themselves as fairly religious or religious, and prayer was among the most common way of coping with stress. African Americans are 20 percent more likely to report having serious psychological distress than whites, according to the US Department of Health and Human Services Office of Minority Services. Yet adult African Americans, especially those with higher levels of education, are less likely to seek mental health services than their white counterparts. Historically, African Americans have normalized their own suffering. During slavery, mental illness often resulted from a more inhumane lifestyle, including frequent beatings and abuse, which forced many slaves to hide their issues. Over time, strength became equated with survival and weakness (including mental illness), which meant you might not survive. That stigma still exists today.

Growing up, I was always told to read the Bible or pray to get over feelings that I now know were depression. In adulthood, I have learned that it is okay to not be okay. African Americans may be resistant to seeking treatment because they fear it may reflect badly on their families—an outward admission of the family's failure to handle problems internally. For many African Americans who suffer from mental disorders, most hold negative attitudes toward people who obtain mental health care. No matter how bad their situation was, they did not want to be one of "those people." Many African Americans, especially those who have ascended the socioeconomic and professional ladder in the face of institutionalized racism, struggle with a feeling of being compelled to be strong. Some are so socially isolated that they feel they cannot trust anyone or share anything and must go it alone.

Mental illness takes many forms; therefore, the issues those battling mental health face often go unseen. For some black celebrities with mental health issues, life is often filled with tragedy and triumphs while engaging in a private and public battle. We go to their concerts and appearances, buy their music, and stay glued to the television for the season's hottest series. We watch African American celebrities and public figures on the world stage entertain and inspire us every day, yet we pay no attention to the signs and symptoms that they are suffering in silence. Only once they spiral out of control, often into total self-destruction, do we begin to wonder if something is wrong. Like many things that influence us, hearing about the challenges with mental illness by celebrities and public figures in our community has been helpful in breaking the silence. Serena Williams, Oprah Winfrey, Dwayne "The Rock" Johnson, and former US Congressman Jesse Jackson Jr. suffered from depression; Michael Jackson was said to have a condition which caused a negative preoccupation with body image; Nina Simone suffered from bipolar disorder, as do Chris Brown, DMX, and Mike Tyson; Don Cornelius committed suicide; even Dr. Martin Luther King Jr. suffered from depression and was suicidal. Kanye West wisely sought, and received, mental health treatment. Is he really that different from the rest of us? Probably not as much as we would like to think. A cultural shift is needed to foster a climate in which friends and loved ones can seek nonjudgmental support for a mental health condition. Education about mental disorders and the treatment process is critical to reducing barriers to treatment among the African American community. Suggestions for overcoming this barrier include public education campaigns, educational presentations at community venues, and open information sessions at local mental health clinics. This could make a difference in helping others feel empowered to get the help they may need. Remember, I am not a doctor. I just sound like one. Take good care of yourself and live the best life possible! isolated that they feel they cannot trust anyone or share anything and must go at it alone. Mental illness takes many forms; therefore, the issues those battling mental health face often go unseen. For some black celebrities with mental health issues, life is often filled with tragedy and triumphs while engaging in a private and public battle. We go to their concerts and appearances; buy their music; stay glued to the television for the season's hottest series. We watch African American celebrities and public figures on the world stages entertain and inspire us every day, yet we pay no attention to the signs and symptoms that they are suffering in silence. Only once they spiral out of control, often into total self-destruction, do we begin to wonder "if something is wrong." Like many things that influence us, hearing about the challenges with mental illness by celebrities and public figures in our community has been helpful in "breaking the silence". Serena Williams, Oprah Winfrey, Dwayne "The Rock" Johnson, and former U.S. Congressman Jesse Jackson, Jr. suffered from depression; Michael Jackson was said to have a

condition which caused a negative preoccupation with body image; Nina Simone suffered from bipolar disorder, as do Chris Brown, DMX, and Mike Tyson; Don Cornelius committed suicide; even Dr. Martin Luther King Jr. suffered from depression and was suicidal. Kanye West wisely sought, and received, mental health treatment. Is he really that different from the rest of us? Probably not as much as we would like to think. A cultural shift is needed to foster a climate in which friends and loved ones can seek non-judgmental support for a mental health condition. Education about mental disorders and the treatment process is critical to reducing barriers to treatment among the African American community. Suggestions for overcoming this barrier include public education campaigns, educational presentations at community venues, and open information sessions at local mental health clinics. This could make the difference in helping others feel empowered to get the help they may need. Remember, I am not a doctor. I just sound like one. Take good care of yourself and live the best life possible!

3

Medical System/Historical Abuse in Black and Brown Communities

Medical System

Many black and brown Americans do not trust their health care providers to act in their best interests. The medical community should care about this collective sense of black distrust in medicine, as it is a major factor in the well-documented health disparities between blacks and whites. Research has shown that minorities are much less likely to report trust in their physicians and hospitals; thus, they are less likely to seek treatment or be compliant with recommended treatment plans (Katrina Armstrong, et al., "Racial/Ethnic Differences in Physician Distrust in the United States," *American Journal for Public Health* 97, no. 7 (2007): 1283–9, doi:10.2105/AJPH.2005.080762). In many cases, when blacks and brown have the same diseases as their white counterparts, blacks are much more likely to die sooner. For instance, blacks are three times more likely to die of asthma than white Americans (US Department of Health and Human Services of Minority Health, "Asthma and African Americans," January 9, 2018, https://minorityhealth.hhs.gov/omh/browse.aspx?lvl=4&lvlid=15). Black and brown have a 25 percent higher cancer death rate than their white counterparts. Black and brown women have a 20 percent higher cancer death rate than white women (National Cancer Institute, "Cancer Disparities, March 11, 2019, cancer.gov, https://www.cancer.gov/about-cancer/understanding/disparities). Blacks tend to develop chronic diseases earlier in life and, overall, have shorter life expectancies when compared to whites ("The Health and Life Expectancy of Older Blacks and Hispanics in the United States" *Today's Research on Aging* 28 (June 2013), https://assets.

prb.org/pdf13/TodaysResearchAging28.pdf). Trust is not only a foundational element to a therapeutic doctor-patient relationship but also is a vital factor in a patient's decision making to seek help. In order to address this distrust in the US health care system, there must be an exploration of the historical roots and how prejudice operates in the modern medical context.

Historical Abuse

Historical Perspective

The US medical establishment has a long legacy of discriminating and exploiting black Americans, the indelible memory of which remains deeply embedded in the collective consciousness of the community. Historically, medicine has used black bodies, without consent, for its own advancement while medical theories, technologies, and institutions were used to reinforce systems of oppression. In the antebellum period, blacks were forced to participate in dissections and medical examinations. Dead black bodies, robbed from their graves, were a continuous source of surgical and anatomical experimentation. The psychiatric diagnosis of drapetomania, or runaway slave syndrome, was created to diagnose and pathologize African slaves who fled their vicious slave owners. To run away from slavery was considered a disease. The treatment was often the amputation of the extremities. Later, during the reconstruction era, white American doctors argued that former slaves would not thrive in a free society because their minds could not cope psychologically with freedom. In the civil rights era, psychiatrists used the concept of schizophrenia to portray black activists as violent, hostile, and paranoid because they threatened the racist status quo. The Tuskegee Syphilis Study, where hundreds of black men, without their consent, were intentionally administered syphilis and denied treatment, became the very embodiment of the way medicine and medical research were weaponized against African Americans. Scholars have written for decades about the Tuskegee experiments symbolizing the racisms embedded in medicine and laying the foundation for the black community's distrust of physicians and research. Many scholars agree that although the black distrust of the health system started way before Tuskegee—this study has become the central metaphor and focal point to explain black distrust in medicine and public health.

In Modern Times

Is it no surprise that black and brown Americans do not trust doctors or hospitals? As health care professionals, this is the cultural and social genealogy that we have inherited. Despite trends in the reduction of racial prejudice in recent decades, the marginalization of black and brown Americans takes place at every level of the contemporary medical system—the prescription patterns at times or the increased restraints used in the hospital and hospital staff insistent that certain black patients were dangerous, requiring four-point restraints, which meant that each of the limbs would be strapped to the bed. In my own research, I have found and experienced that black Americans with mental health diagnoses are less likely to receive certain medicines for their conditions compared to whites with the same condition. Blacks are less likely to be prescribed newer, better-tolerated medicine called atypical antipsychotics (Laurel A. Copeland, et al., "Racial disparity in the use of atypical antipsychotic medications among veterans," *The American Journal of Psychiatry* 160, no. 10 (2003): 1817–22, doi: 10.1176/appi.ajp.160.10.1817). Rather, they tend to be offered older medicine with worse side effects. Specifically, a drug called Clozapine, which is considered the Cadillac of psychiatric medicine because of its superior effectiveness, is prescribed less to minority patients with serious mental illness when compared to white patients (Deanna L. Kelly, et al. "Clozapine utilization and outcomes by race in a public mental health system: 1994–2000," *Journal of Clinical Psychiatry* 67, no. 9 (2006): 1404–11, doi: 10.4088/jcp.v67n0911). From the time a person enters the waiting area of an emergency room or clinic to the time spent with the doctor, as well as the doctor's treatment, decision-making is all influenced by race and ethnicity. One study of emergency room records indicates that black patients are more likely than whites to receive lower triage scores for the same complaints, meaning that triage personnel rate the complaints as less serious (Chet D. Schrader and Lawrence M. Lewis, "Racial disparity in emergency department triage," *Journal of Emergency Medicine* 44, no. 2 (2013): 11–8, doi: 10.1016/j.jemermed.2012.05.010). As a result, less serious complaints in emergency rooms translates into longer wait times. Even in case of a serious medical emergency, such as in the case of stroke, where time for intervention is critical, blacks experience long wait time for stroke medications (Sudeep J. Karve, et al., "Racial/ethnic disparities in emergency department waiting time for stroke patients in the United States," *Journal of Stroke and Cerebrovascular Diseases* 20, no. 1 (2011): 30–40, doi: 10.1016/j.jstrokecerebrovasdis.2009.10.006). After long wait times, when minority patients are finally able to even see a physician, several studies have shown that physicians spend less time with blacks patients when compared to whites and are less likely to perceive the patient as being honest regarding their symptoms (Shaun M. Eack, et al., "Interviewer-Perceived Honesty Mediates Racial Disparities in the Diagnosis of Schizophrenia," *Psychiatric Services* 63, no.9 (2012): 875–880, doi: 10.1176/appi.ps.201100388).

The medical community must address the real sense of suspicion, distrust, and cynicism that is deeply embedded in the black's collective memory. Earning a patient's trust is a very difficult feat given these historical forces, but medical education systems, hospitals, and physicians themselves can take steps to address this issue. First, physicians, hospitals, and schools can address the role of implicit racial bias, which is often described as automatically activated and often unintentional. Implicit racial bias has proved to be a powerful, validated tool to help explain health care disparities. For instance, in one study, doctors who were found to have higher levels of implicit bias (as measure by the implicit-association test of Harvard University were more likely to withhold treatment from a black patient (Alexander R. Green, et al., "Implicit bias among physicians and its prediction of thrombolysis decisions for black and white patients," *Journal of General Internal Medicine* 22, no. 9 (2007): 1231–8, doi: 10.1007/s11606-007-0258-5). The schools of medicine can do its part in ensuring doctors are properly trained by integrating the concept of implicit bias into medical education curriculums. Health care organizations should also offer training to health care professionals to address implicit Wisconsin-Madison, have understood implicit bias to be a habit of the mind, and can be changed over time, if the person is aware, concerned, and interventions are employed to replace the bias (Patricia G. Devine, et al., "Long-term reduction in implicit race bias: A prejudice habit-breaking intervention," *Journal of Experimental Psychology* 48, no. 6 (2012): 1267–1278, doi: 10.1016/j.jesp.2012.06.003). It must be acknowledged that gaps in health care disparities result from a myriad of other social determinants of health, such as education level, employment, housing, community recourses, and healthy eating. For this reason, holding policymakers accountable to ensure universal equity to a variety of social resources will prove to be effective in improving the health of the black communities as well. Efforts to improve the health outcomes of black Americans must acknowledge the brutal history and shadow cast by decades of discrimination and the resultant collective distrust by the community.

4

Faith and Spirituality versus Mental Health Care in Black and Brown Communities

Depression looks different for black and brown Americans. What happens we are undiagnosed by professional health care? Most families in minority communities rely on faith, the church, and spiritual beliefs for emotional strength and support instead of seeking professional help for their mental health rather than turning to health care professionals. Faith and spirituality can help in the recovery process but should not be the only option you pursue. If your spirituality is an important part of your life, your spiritual practices can be a strong part of your treatment plan. Be aware that, sometimes, faith churches can be a source of distress and stigma if they are misinformed about mental health or do not know how to support families dealing with these conditions. A connection to faith has been recognized as having a deeply profound impact on emotional well-being. Throughout history, a connection to a higher power has been the cornerstone of the resilience and empowerment that has sustained generations of individuals during the African diaspora. Trauma and health disparities faced both historically and currently by the black and brown people contribute to the enduring legacy of faith/spirituality. To this day, it remains a powerful source of hope for the community. The church is the first choice for many individuals in times of personal distress. Having a conversation with a trusted community leader, who is aware of cultural concerns, can improve the mental wellness of individuals and families. Encouraging the mental health and faith communities to mentally learn from and respect one another is a progressive and necessary step in the right direction. Everyone deserves an equal opportunity to offer their gifts, talents, and strength to the community. Faith communities should not replace trained mental health service providers but work to support them. Faith leaders should seek opportunities to collaborate and work together to help the communities and their families. Studies indicate that the outcome of psychotherapy in religious patients can be enhanced by integrating religious elements into the therapy protocol and by nonreligious therapists alike.

The following are a few helpful tips for faith leaders:

- Realize that mental health conditions are medical conditions that are very common.
- It is very likely that several families in your congregation are impacted by mental health issues in some way or another, which makes mental health a significant concern of the entire church.
- Mental health conditions are like all other medical conditions and should be treated as such.
- The individuals and families seeking your guidance deserve to have their needs address appropriately even if it means stepping outside of religion and into professional health care.

Misconceptions about Mental Illness

1. People with mental health conditions are unsafe

    Most people with mental illness are peaceful and respectful of other people. The contribution of people with mental illness to overall rates of violence is small. The magnitude of the relationship is greatly exaggerated. Some people with mental illness may have trouble relating to others. Embrace the challenge of interacting with a human being who may have had more struggles in life than you.

2. People with mental illness are unpredictable and difficult to relate to

    Many people with mental illness have professional jobs and are raising stable families. When someone is unwell physically, they are unpredictable, just like a person who is mentally unwell. This is not their normal way of interacting, and many people have a plan in case they become unwell and unpredictable. Give someone the benefit of the doubt. Assume they will be dependable. Show up to meetings and relate with a mentally ill person.

3. Most people with mental illness are on welfare or are homeless

    Most people with mental illness are *not* homeless or on welfare despite the fact that they are in the minority. Yes, there are people who are homeless who suffer from paranoia, delusion, and other mental disorders. Strong people are weak too; even the strongest person can get exhausted. Even the bravest and the most resilient ones can get tired of taking care of themselves and everyone else. Even they can get tired of the independent life they choose to live, of all the bills they need to pay, and of all the work they need to do! Even they get tired of having everyone count on them while not having anyone to count on. Even the strongest need help before breaking down.

4. People with mental illness would rather not talk about it

    This conversation depends on the person, and some people are very open while others are more private.

    What happens when black and brown Americans are undiagnosed by professional health care?

    How many people in the prison system have undiagnosed or untreated mental health issues and how that contributes to them winding back in prison? How many black and brown kids are the product of the juvenile criminal system instead of actually getting them help? Black-on-black crime is at an all-time thing because traumatized victims in turn become homicidal or suicidal. There is a lot to address when you delve into this issue of mental health in the African American community; there are a lot of things that we must overcome. But at the end of the day, it starts with us. At least, be able to talk about our mental health issues, and then we can begin to address them. Untreated depression can lead to not only violence and other mental health issues but also suicide. Our race can get so violent; a person can become homicidal and not even know it. The black community suffers from an increased rate of mental health concerns. The increase in the incidence of psychological difficulties is the black community's lack of ass to appropriate a culturally responsive mental health care.

5

Mental Health Advocate: Taraji P. Henson

Taraji P. Henson says black communities are not getting the mental health care they need. We do not talk enough about mental health in the African American community, and staying quiet is not helping us heal. People in the black and brown communities have long been afraid to talk about our mental health; we just do not do it. We are told to pray it away, we are told to be strong, and we're told it's a sign of weakness or, a lot of times, mental health issues come off as rage and are dismissed or ignored. There are shame and taboo around the topic. We have to break that silence. What made Taraji comfortable in talking about the topic was her father, who had issues with mental illness. She never thought there was something wrong with either having mental health challenges or talking about it. But then when she grew up and had her own hardships, her own trauma, and it was time to deal with them head on, she knew there was an issue. It was not easy for her to talk to a therapist who really understood her challenges as an African American woman. Untreated depression could lead to severe mental illness. It gets so bad to where you become suicidal or homicidal. Because mental illness is not talked about in our community, people do not seek it out as a career option. So we do not have a lot of therapists out there, and those who practice are not easy to find. Taraji P. Henson wants to change that, and I am here to bring awareness. She says, "Beyond that," in terms of looking for a therapist. It is not even about color or culture but about a therapist being culturally competent. Cultural competence means knowing, understanding, and honoring the history of someone. For instance, you might not know exactly what it is like to live in a crack-infested neighborhood, but you need to understand what that does to a family structure. If you blame any systemic issues that are happening to a culture on the individual, you will not be able to guide them properly. Taraji does not feel safe expressing herself to a therapist if she feels like the therapist does not understand her background and her struggles as a black woman. Taraji realized she can help so many people, so she built a foundation. The Boris Lawrence Henson Foundation was born out of that need. The director of the foundation did the research and found the statistic: one in five Americans has a mental illness, but African Americans are the least likely to seek treatment and have a long history of being misdiagnosed. In addition to trying to combat the stigma against the mental care of the black and brown people.

Celebrity Talk

Taraji P. Henson has three major goals:

1. Get more therapists and mental health programs in urban schools. We need professionals in the school systems to recognize when kids are coming from a traumatic experience and how it impacts their ability to learn. For instance, when Taraji was a substitute teacher for children with disabilities, the first time she went to Compton, she pulled up to the school, and the kids were coming up to her, pointing to the bullet holes in the schools and saying, "Ms. Henson, look. It was a shootout last night." That is not normal, but they were expected to go to school in that environment like it was nothing with no counselors, no support. And then, she was put in a class with young boys, all black, who told her that they can't learn because they are special ed. She had been thinking she was there to teach the kids who had mental and physical disabilities, but those kids could read and walk, and they all had their faculties. They have been classified as special education in a school without counselors, in an environment that was clearly traumatic, and in a community where there was limited access to mental health services, and they were told they could not achieve academically. There are so many kids like that. They have nowhere to vent

about these traumatic incidents, and we are expecting them to just go to school and learn. We need help too in that area.

In direct response to this, Taraji's foundation recently partnered with nonprofit organizations to bring young mental health first-aid training to teachers and staff, as well as workshops to develop a trauma-informed curriculum. Her partners offer tools to recognize and address children coming from traumatic situations, as well as know what to do to get them some help or some kind of relief.

2. Increase the number of African American mental health providers by normalizing the conversation around mental health with young people at an early age, piquing their interest and making it cool to want to be a psychologist, therapist, or counselor. Her foundation is also giving scholarships for students pursuing a career in the mental health field.

3. Addressing recidivism in the prison system

    The foundation partnering with organizations that offer programs that help formerly incarcerated people have access to mental health services and assist them in the reintegration process into the community. Many people do not realize

Celebrity Talk

Mental Health Awareness by Black/Brown Celebrities

We watch African American celebrities and public figures on the world stages entertain and inspire us every day, yet we pay no attention to the signs and symptoms that they are suffering in silence. Only once they have spiraled out of control, often into total self-destruction, do we begin to wonder if something is wrong. Like many things that influence us, hearing about the challenges with mental illness by celebrities and public figures in our community has been helpful in breaking the silence. Serena Williams, Oprah Winfrey, Dwayne "The Rock" Johnson, and former US Congressman Jesse Jackson Jr. suffered from depression; Michael Jackson was said to have a condition which caused a negative preoccupation with body image; Nina Simone suffered from bipolar disorder, as do Chris Brown, DMX, and Mike Tyson; Don Cornelius committed suicide; even Dr. Martin Luther King Jr. suffered from depression and was suicidal. Kanye West wisely sought, and received, mental health treatment. Is he really that different from the rest of us? Probably not as much as we would like to think. A cultural shift is needed to foster a climate in which friends and loved ones can seek non-judgmental support for a mental health condition. Education about mental disorders and the treatment process is critical in reducing the barriers to treatment among the African American community. Suggestions for overcoming this barrier include public education campaigns, educational presentations at community venues, and open information sessions at local mental health clinics. This could make a difference in helping others feel empowered to get the help they may need. Remember, I am not a doctor. I just sound like one. Take good care of yourself and live the best life possible!

Celebrity Beyoncé speaks up on her struggles with mental health. When it comes to wellness, the topic of mental health, though still stigmatized, is slowly gaining popularity. With stars such as Beyoncé, Dwayne "The Rock" Johnson, Kerry Washington, and Kanye West opening up about their struggles with depression and anxiety, many more people are able to speak up about mental health. According to the World Health Organization, one in four people suffers from mental illness. The statistics also show that more women are prone to suffering from anxiety.

6

Homicidal versus Suicidal: The White versus Black Youth in Black and Brown Communities

Study: Young Black Children Have Higher Suicide Rates than Whites

Tala Salem, *USNews*, May 21, 2018, https://www.usnews.com/news/health-care-news/articles/2018-05-21/study-young-black-children-have-higher-suicide-rates-than-whites

Black children have higher suicide rates than white children at younger ages, but those proportions flip in the teenage years, according to a new study that challenges commonly held beliefs about racial disparities in child suicide rates. The study, published Monday in the journal *JAMA Pediatrics* and based on an analysis of suicide rates among children aged 5 to 17 between 2001 and 2015, found suicide rates were 42 percent lower overall among black youths than white youths. But among children aged 5 to 12, black children had a significantly higher incidence of suicide than white children. From 13 to 17, the suicide rate was lower among black children than white children. This is an important finding because it's widely believed suicide rates in white individuals are higher across the lifespan than black individuals," Dr. Jeff Bridge, the study's lead author, says. "Traditionally, (suicide rates in whites) have been higher, but in the last decade and a half there's been a reversal in that phenomenon." The suicide rate among black children under 13 was approximately double that of white children, a finding observed in both boys and girls. But for youth aged 13 to 17, it was roughly 50 percent lower in black children than in white children. From 2001 to 2015, officials recorded 1,661 suicide deaths in black children and 13,341 suicide deaths in white children aged 5 to 17 years in the U.S. Although the findings highlight opportunities for targeted prevention efforts, data is limited and researchers could not identify factors that explain age-related race differences in suicide, including access to culturally acceptable behavioral health care or the potential role of death due to homicide among black adolescents, according to the study. However, the findings highlight the significance of exploring race-related differences in suicide and developing more effective suicide detection and prevention efforts for both black and white children at different stages of their childhood and adolescence, according to Bridge. The Centers for Disease Control and Prevention often uses five-year or 10-year age bands for analyzing data on suicide rates. For children, according to Bridge, the CDC should be considering developmental periods as opposed to age bands. "Had we analyzed data that way, we would not have found age-related racial disparities," he says. That is because suicide rates increase throughout each age of adolescence, Bridge says, and every year a child gets older the suicide rate increases until the age of adulthood. "Going forward, surveillance efforts need to reflect the association between age and suicide," Bridge says. "We can't just rely on age groupings across five-year developmental periods. When the CDC publishes statistics, the groupings cut across large developmental periods and that runs the risk of missing some age-related differences in the risk for suicide."

Suicide rates for black children twice that of white children, new data show

Amy Ellis Nutt, *The Washington Post*, May 22, 2018, https://www.washingtonpost.com/news/to-your-health/wp/2018/05/21/suicide-rates-for-black-children-twice-that-of-white-children-new-data-show/

Although suicide is rare among young children, the latest findings reinforce the need for better research into the racial disparities, lead author Jeffrey Bridge said Monday. Suicide is one of the leading causes of death for older children and adolescents in the United States. "We can't assume any longer that suicide rates are uniformly higher in white individuals than black," said Bridge, an epidemiologist who directs the Center for Suicide Prevention and Research at the Columbus hospital. "There is this age-related disparity, and now we have to understand the underlying reasons.... Most of the previous research has largely concerned white suicide. So we don't even know if the same risk and protective factors apply to black youth." Historically, suicide rates in the United States have been higher for whites than blacks across all age groups. That remains the case for adolescents, ages 13 to 17, according to the new study. White teens continue to have a 50 percent higher rate of suicide than black teens. Overall, between 1999 and 2015, more than 1,300 children ages 5 to 12 took their own lives in the United States, according to the Centers for Disease Control and Prevention. Those numbers translate into an average of one child 12 or younger dying by suicide every five days. The pace has actually accelerated in recent years, CDC statistics indicate. The researchers based their latest analysis on the CDC's Web-based Injury Statistics Query and Reporting System, which does not include geographical or socioeconomic data. Although the study was unable to provide a cultural context for the racial difference in suicide rates, psychiatrist Samoon Ahmad thinks a number of reasons could account for the disparity. "To Amy, the 5–12 range is more related to developmental issues and the possible lack of a family network, social network and cultural activities," said Ahmad, a clinical associate professor at the NYU School of Medicine who was not involved in the research. "And with the introduction of social media, there is more isolation with children, not as much neighborhood play. Kids are more socially in their own vacuum." Ahmad described this age group as "probably the most vulnerable." Yet adults tend to think the children are somehow too young to experience such depths of despair, he noted. "No one talks about that with them. We tend to put them in silos, and don't discuss these things because we think it's too traumatic," he said. "Instead, there must be a slow and steady flow of communication." Previous studies have looked at some of the characteristics and circumstances surrounding children's suicides. In 2017, research by Bridge and colleagues found that among children, ages 5 to 11, and young adolescents, ages 12 to 14, those who took their own lives were more likely to be male, African American and dealing with stressful relationships at home or with friends. Children who had a mental health problem at the time of death were more likely than young adolescents to have been diagnosed with attention-deficit disorder or attention-deficit hyperactivity disorder. Young adolescents who killed themselves were more likely to have had relationship problems with a boyfriend or girlfriend. They also had higher rates of depression, according to last year's study, which was published in the journal Pediatrics. That 2017 report found more than a third of elementary school-aged suicides involved black children compared to just 11.6 percent of early adolescent suicides. Bridge said his motivation for delving into this issue was a suicide in a town not far from Columbus. The child was not yet "We went into the original study because suicide rates were increasing among adolescents in the United States," Bridge said. The local death "made us think if there was a change in the suicide rate of children, and that's what made us look into it."

National Alliance on Mental Illness (NAMI) in Black and Brown Communities

Racial Disparities in Mental Health and Criminal Justice

Leah Pope, National Alliance of Mental Illness (NAMI), July 24, 2019, https://www.nami.org/Blogs/NAMI-Blog/July-2019/Racial-Disparities-in-Mental-Health-and-Criminal-Justice

July is Minority Mental Health Month, a time dedicated to raising awareness about the unique challenges that underrepresented communities face in accessing mental health treatment in the U.S.

The Problem

The overrepresentation of people of color—especially black people—in the criminal justice system is a well-established fact. Vera's Arrest Trends tool—which maps annual, nationwide arrest data—shows that black people were 2.17 times more likely to be arrested than white people in 2016. Our Incarceration Trends tool shows even greater racial disparities, with black people being 3.5 times more likely to be incarcerated in jail and nearly five times more likely to be incarcerated in prison nationwide.

It is also widely known that people with mental illness are overrepresented in the criminal justice system. The most recent data available from the Bureau of Justice Statistics shows that more than one quarter of people in jail met the threshold for serious psychological distress and nearly half had been told by a mental health professional that they have a mental illness. What's troubling is that even though people of color are more likely to be involved in the criminal justice system, there is evidence that they are less likely to be identified as having a mental health problem. Also, they are less likely to receive access to treatment once incarcerated. There is also substantial evidence of racial and ethnic disparities in community mental health care. As documented by the U.S. surgeon general's report on mental health, racial and ethnic minorities have less access to mental health services than white people, are less likely to receive needed care and are more likely to receive poor-quality care when they are treated.

Additionally, there may be unique dynamics at play once people enter the criminal justice system that contribute to even greater racial disparities in the screening, evaluation, diagnosis, and treatment of people with mental health problems. For example, there is evidence that prosecutors are more likely to grant pretrial diversion to white defendants than to black or Latinx defendants with similar legal characteristics. This could have especially negative effects for people of color with mental illness since pretrial jail incarceration has significant negative health impacts. Other evidence shows that mental health screening tools used by jails reproduce racial disparities, resulting in fewer black and Latinx people screening positive and thus remaining under-referred and undetected in the jail population. Incarceration itself also impacts important factors of health, such as housing. Formerly incarcerated people are nearly 10 times more likely to be homeless, and rates of homelessness are especially high among people of color. Lack of housing can significantly worsen mental health problems.

The Solution

The good news is that there is increased focus on how to divert people with mental illness—including people of color with mental illness—out of the criminal justice system entirely. Jurisdictions across the country are developing and implementing models to improve responses to people with mental illness. There is widespread agreement around the need to improve police responses to people with mental illness and to create diversion programs that link people to community-based treatment instead of incarceration. As one example of the current progress, Vera launched Serving Safely last year through support from the Bureau of Justice Assistance and in collaboration with partner organizations, including NAMI. Serving Safely is a national initiative to improve law enforcement responses to people with mental illness and intellectual and developmental disabilities. To date, we have provided training and technical assistance to more than 50 police departments, prosecutors' offices, and public safety communications representatives (911 call-takers and dispatchers) across the country. Among our many activities, we are educating departments about the variety of models to successfully respond to people in crisis. And we are supporting NAMI to develop a training course that coaches peers to make effective presentations to law enforcement. Serving Safely is one concrete example of the effort to raise awareness about the overrepresentation of people with mental illnesses in the criminal justice system. We need to both reduce contact and improve interactions for people at the earliest stage of justice-system involvement. Helping law enforcement officers improve their responses provides important opportunities to lessen the health disparities that are so rooted in our justice system. But continued progress requires that the interventions being developed and implemented across the country be done so with an eye toward—and a commitment to—reducing racial disparities. Without a conscious commitment to racial equity in this work, communities risk recreating patterns of unequal justice even as they strive to improve responses to people with mental illness. Indeed, advancing racial equity is a commitment that must go hand-in-hand with reform to both the criminal justice system and the mental health system.

Jail versus Mental Institution in Black and Brown Communities

Mental Illness and Jails: Race Is Left Out of the Equation

James Kilgore, *Prison Legal News*, July 13, 2015, https://www.prisonlegalnews.org/news/2015/jul/13/mental-illness-and-jails-race-left-out-equation/

In 1843, social justice crusader Dorothea Dix went before the Massachusetts Legislature with the intention of addressing an acute problem of the day: the incarceration of people with mental illness. Her declaration to the assembly highlighted the "state of Insane Persons," protesting that they were confined "in cages, stalls, pens! Chained, naked, beaten with rods, and lashed into obedience." Her efforts led to the creation of the state's first mental health hospitals. For the next several years, Dix travelled from state to state, repeating her cycle of advocating for special facilities for people living with mentally illness apart from jails and prisons. Though she was successful in many states, her work now stands as ancient history. When it comes to mental health, we have retreated back to the days of the "cages, stalls and pens."

Racism pervades the prison industrial complex. No serious attempt at reform can ignore this (italics added).

In many communities, jails have become the only option for police confronted with a person in mental health crisis in public. The reason behind this is obvious: the virtual shutdown of the nation's public mental health care system for which Dix fought. From 1970 to 2002, the per capita number of public mental health hospital beds plummeted from 207 per 100,000 to 20 per 100,000. The intent of these closures was to dismantle large, often punitive mental institutions and replace them with community-based facilities that would have a more patient-centered ethos. Unfortunately, these closures took place at a moment when neoliberalism was on the rise. In the name of fiscal responsibility, most states simply did not replace mental health institutions. In many instances, jails became the quick fix to handle poor people who had mental health crises and no access to treatment. By 2004, a Department of Justice survey found that 64 percent of local jail populations and 56 percent of those in prisons had symptoms of mental illness. More recent studies cited in a 2014 report by the National Research Council show no abatement of this situation. The presence of mental illness among incarcerated women is particularly acute. A 2009 survey of Maryland and New York jails showed that 31 percent of women had serious mental illnesses, more than double the rate for men. Though no Dorothea Dix figure has emerged in 2015, at long last policy makers and researchers are waking up to the issue. More than 50 counties, including Champaign, Illinois, where I live, have passed a resolution circulated by the Council on State Governments, backing treatment in the community rather than incarceration. This resolution, part of an initiative called "Stepping Up," comes on the heels of major research reports by Human Rights Watch and the Urban Institute on the challenges of mental illness in jails and prisons. While attention to this problem is long overdue, the framing of Stepping Up as well as the work by Human Rights Watch and the Urban Institute suffers from a common but crucial blind spot: no mention of race. As Michelle Alexander and others have tirelessly pointed out, racism pervades the prison industrial complex. No serious attempt at reform, let alone transformation, can ignore this.

Overlooked Issues of Race

In the intersection between mental health and incarceration, at least four racial issues surface. First, the petition and recent reports present a static model of the relationship between mental health and incarceration. The assumed dynamic holds that people have pre-existing mental health issues, which get misinterpreted as criminality, resulting in arrest and lockup. The cure then becomes putting people into treatment rather than behind bars. While choosing treatment over incarceration may represent a step forward, policy makers and practitioners need to dig deeper into the complex root causes of mental illness. Often, treatment is far from enough. Mental illness can be the product of individual circumstances – a traumatic event, a person's brain chemistry or even their genetic makeup. However, a considerable body of research links many instances of mental illness to experiences of poverty and violence, which are disproportionate realities in poor communities of color. Researcher Jack Carney outlines the relationship between poverty and mental illness in his provocatively titled article, "Poverty and Mental Illness: You Can't Have One Without the Other." Indeed, the violence of poverty can often trigger poor mental health. People may have mental illness because they have grown up without sufficient nutrition or without access to adequate education, housing, or career opportunities. Mental illness may also be precipitated by an environment where fear of racialized police violence, deportation or domestic abuse is a constant reality. These are structural problems which medication, therapy groups or wraparound services cannot reverse. As "Elizabeth," a homeless Massachusetts woman with a history of mental health problems, told Susan Sered, a Suffolk University professor, "I don't need to talk about my problems. I need a place to live so that I won't be scared all of the time."

Mass incarceration . . . has exacerbated and further racialized the problems of mental illness. It is both cause and effect (italics added).

The Trauma of Incarceration

Secondly, mass incarceration, which disproportionately impacts poor people of color, has exacerbated, and further racialized the problems of mental illness. It is both cause and effect. Cycling in and out of prisons and jails is traumatic, often undermining prospects for economic and social stability. Long-term incarceration, especially in high security or supermax facilities, accentuates the problem. All of this has worsened due to the cutbacks in education and job training programs in prison in the last three decades, heightening the possibility of depression while incarcerated and lack of opportunity after release.

In addition, offering quality mental health treatment in prisons and jails can be difficult. On the one hand, as psychology professor Craig Haney has noted, "prisoners are reluctant to open up in environments where they do not feel physically or psychologically safe." On the other, institutional realities—violence, poor food, lockdowns, isolation, and racial discrimination—further inhibit progress for mental health patients. As James Pleasant, currently finishing his 13th year of incarceration in Minnesota, said, "Sleeping on a concrete slab will not solve mental health issues." Even if treatment is effective, Haney argues that the transition to care outside of prisons is frequently "spotty" because there's not an effective pass-off to the service providers in the community. Some war veterans and survivors of violent attacks may qualify for PTSD therapy, but such services are rarely available to those suffering from post-incarceration stress. They are left to cope for themselves, generally with very few resources.

Racial Stereotyping and a Lack of Cultural Competency

A third key issue is racial stereotyping. This takes several forms. At the level of day-to-day police responses, Dr. Tiffany Townsend, a senior director in the American Psychological Association's Public Interest Directorate, has stressed that Black people are "more likely to be ushered into the criminal justice system" as opposed to being placed in treatment. In other cases, stereotyping can have even more serious consequences. The cases of Ezell Ford in Los Angeles, Lavall Hall in Miami Gardens and Michelle Cusseaux in Phoenix, all killed by police, constitute evidence that Black individuals in mental health crises run serious risks of being criminalized and "treated" with fatal gunfire rather than de-escalation or crisis intervention techniques. Lastly, mental health treatment, both within carceral institutions and beyond, reflects the greater racial politics of society at large. From the days of diagnosing runaway enslaved people with an affliction called drapetomania in the 1800s to the labeling of Black protesters in the 1960s as schizophrenic, the mental health establishment has a considerable legacy of racist practice. This history still impacts the attitudes of both mental health practitioners and patients. In 1999, a surgeon general's report noted the inferiority of mental health services provided to people of color. A 2014 research team from Morehouse College of Medicine showed that the problems persist. Such disparities are reinforced by the lack of people of color, especially African Americans, among mental health care professionals. According to a recent article posted by the National Alliance on Mental Illness, Black people make up just 3.7 percent of members in the American Psychiatric Association and 1.5 percent of those in the American Psychological Association. Black psychologist Dr. Josephine Johnson argues that "cultural competency," which the National Institutes of Health define as "the ability to deliver services that are respectful of and responsive to the health beliefs, practices and cultural and linguistic needs of diverse patients," is an "ethical mandate." Cultural competency of care providers for those who have were involved with the criminal legal system may be especially critical for those who have had negative experiences with white authority figures along the street-to-prison pipeline. The lack of cultural competency appears in the carceral setting as well. In an interview with *Truthout*, Melissa Thompson, a professor at Portland State University, said that in researching her book *Mad or Bad? Race, Class, Gender, and Mental Disorder in the Criminal Justice System*, she found racial disparities between Black people and white people "quite pervasive." She carried out both in an intensive study of Hennepin County Jail in Minnesota and a review of national data. She cited racial differences in regard to mental health relating to how people were charged, their access to and quality of treatment received in prisons and jails as well as conditions of probation and parole. These differences even remained when she "confined her analysis to those who self-identified as mentally ill."

Mental Health Support or Medical Control?

Finally, even if present efforts in carceral mental health do develop a racial consciousness, it may not be enough. Some researchers fear we may be shifting from one punishment paradigm to another, as some people describe it, from a prison industrial complex to a "treatment-industrial complex." Sociologist Susan Sered expressed the concern to Truthout that the transition from "criminal" to "mentally ill" points to a change in status from "someone who did something bad and can serve his or her debt to society" to "someone who is fundamentally and permanently sick." In her view, an uncaring or poorly conceptualized mental health "alternative" could end up looking much more like medical control and even experimentation rather than a genuine transformation of public policy and invigoration of the communities that have been devastated by mass incarceration and criminalization of their populations. Hence, while the call for reducing the population of people living with mentally illness in jails is timely and necessary, advocates of mental health incarceration need to embrace a more nuanced analysis of the intersection between race, mental illness, and incarceration. Without this, little substantive change is likely to result.

21 Harsh Truths Black People Don't Want to Hear

"There is a separation happening amongst us. Those of us that are "awake" becoming "awake" are slowing and quietly moving away from the rest who *insist* on remaining asleep."

This disjointment, which I simply call Negro Madness Disease, will either stop just in time for the revolution to begin or it will hinder us in our struggle. I hope this harsh but well-intentioned post will cause you to think, pause and ask yourselves, "Is this what the ancestors died for?"

1. Your own jealousies, competitiveness, in-fighting, unwillingness to support one another and pettiness with other black people is what's keeping you from moving forward. (Pssssst! White people are masters at The Brown vs. Brown Game)

2. We *never* learn from history because we believe:

    a. That white people can change

    b. That things are "getting better"

    c. God will help us if we just pray and do nothing to help ourselves

    d. That just because *we* lack the capacity for evil, others lack it too.

3. the latest gadget, like a 50" flat Having screen TV for showing off, is more important than building stronger communities.

4. Eurocentric education is by far the worst thing that has ever happened to us:

5. No matter how big your house, how fancy your car and how expensive your jewelry, whites are not EVER going to be impressed with you or have respect for you. To them, you are just another nigger.

6. Treating each other like garbage isn't going to win you favors with whites.

7. We kill each other because we can't kill the enemy.

8. Most other Colored's, especially those with direct African blood, don't want anything to do with us for they are ashamed to be labeled with us.

9. The reason why we fight each other is because we hate ourselves.

10. Identifying with white people is the foundation for our mental illness:

11. All black people are mentally ill, but we don't want to accept it.

12. We latch on to other people's struggles as a way to get them to accept us . . . which they NEVER do.

13. Black men who hate black women hate themselves.

14. Black women who hate black men have no self-respect.

15. The fact that our children are being led astray is our fault.

16. The black church is the white man's most effective weapon.

17. Whites despise us with a blinding passion because they need something, we have

18. We are still waiting to be told how to fix "the problem with no name" because we are too passive and complacent to figure it out ourselves (https://diaryofanegress.com/2012/10/13/7-easy-steps-to-help-counter-white-supremacy/).

19. Marrying dating and sleeping with a white person will *never* change the color of your skin. Will *never* gain you acceptance into the White Club and will *never* stop them from calling you a no-good, low-down, dirty Nigger:

20. If whites had the chance, tomorrow morning slavery would be back with a vengeance...and they would make sure it remains in existence for all eternity. Accept it.

21. We have no friends/allies on this planet.

7

Research on Inequality in the Health Care System

Racism, Inequality, and Health Care for African Americans

Dr. Jamila K. Taylor, The Century Foundation,
December 19, 2019, https://tcf.org/content/report/
racism-inequality-health-care-african-americans/

Dr. Jamila K. Taylor is director of health care reform and senior fellow at The Century Foundation, where she leads TCF's work to build on the Affordable Care Act and develop the next generation of health reform to achieve high-quality, affordable, and universal coverage in America. She thinks the American health care system in beset with inequalities that have a disproportionate impact on people of color and other marginalized groups. These inequalities contribute to gaps in health insurance coverage, uneven access to services, and poorer health outcomes among certain populations. African Americans bear the brunt of these health care challenges. African Americans comprise 13.4 percent of the US population. Over the span of several decades, namely since the Civil Rights Acts of 1964 and 1968, they have been able to make notable strides in American society. According to the Economic Policy Institute, educational attainment has greatly increased, with more than 90 percent of African Americans aged 25–29 having graduated from high school. College graduation rates have also improved among African Americans. When it comes to income, gains have been made as well, but African Americans are still paid less than white Americans for the same jobs and lag significantly behind when it comes to accumulating wealth. And as for home ownership, just over 40 percent of African Americans own a home—a rate virtually unchanged since 1968. African Americans are also living longer, and the majority of them have some form of health insurance coverage. However, African Americans still experience illness and infirmity at extremely high rates and have lower life expectancy than other racial and ethnic groups. They are also one of the poorest demographics in this country. This report will examine the state of health care coverage for African Americans and shed a light on important social factors that uniquely impact their health outcomes. In an effort to draw implications from leading health care reform plans, recommendations are made for the way forward in ensuring that the physiological and social impacts of racism are not omitted in efforts to secure truly universal health care coverage in America. African Americans are one of the most politically engaged demographics in this country. Addressing their unique challenges and perspectives, including the pervasive impacts of racism, must be included in health reform efforts.

Coverage Gains—and Obstacles—for African Americans Under the ACA

The Affordable Care Act (ACA) has helped to ensure health care coverage for millions of Americans. The uninsured rate among African Americans declined after the law was implemented: of the more than 20 million people who have gained coverage under the ACA, 2.8 million of them are African-American.4 Yet this population is still more likely to be uninsured than white Americans: as of 2018, the uninsured rate among African Americans was 9.7 percent, while it was just 5.4 percent among whites. African Americans were more likely to be covered through employer-sponsored or private health insurance: 55 percent of African Americans used private health insurance in 2018, while 41.2 percent were enrolled in Medicaid or some other type of public health insurance. While coverage expansions under the ACA have hastened the progress toward universal coverage, the continued high cost of many coverage options means that access to affordable health care is still a challenge for many Americans—particularly African Americans. The average family spends $8,200 (or 11 percent of family income) per year on health care premiums, and out-of-pocket costs for things such as office visit copays, prescription drugs, and surprise or out of plan medical bills continue to wreak havoc on the financial security of families. For African Americans, the average annual cost for health care premiums is almost 20 percent8 of the average household income—a major cost to bear, when taking into account income inequality and other economic challenges for this demographic. The high cost of coverage has kept the number of uninsured and underinsured unacceptably high: of the 27.5 million people that still lack health insurance coverage, 45 percent cite cost as the reason for being uninsured. Furthermore, the Commonwealth Fund estimates that an additional 87 million people (adults aged 19 to 64) are underinsured; that is, they have coverage, but their plan leads to unusually high out-of-pocket costs relative to income that can lead to a strain on personal finances or even debt. Of these underinsured adults, 18 percent are African American.

Systemic Health Care Challenges That Reform Must Address

Despite coverage gains, remaining health care challenges exist that have a disproportionate impact on African Americans. The lack of Medicaid expansion in key states, health disparities, and health care provider shortages make it incredibly hard to address America's health care needs in a comprehensive way. And while these challenges are factors that touch many Americans in various parts of the country, the gravity of them is uniquely seen in the South, and among the African American population.

The South's Stubborn Approach to Medicaid Expansion

The Medicaid program has been a lifeline for low-income Americans, pregnant people, the elderly, and people with disabilities. It is jointly funded by states and the federal government and has been operating for fifty-four years. As of August 2019, the program covered 68 million people, with African Americans making up about

20 percent of Medicaid enrollees. Because African Americans tend to be poorer than other demographic groups on average, public health insurance programs such as Medicaid are vital to ensure affordable health care and healthier outcomes. In states that have not expanded Medicaid under the Affordable Care Act (ACA), African Americans and other people of color are most likely to fall within a coverage gap—meaning they earn too much to qualify for the traditional Medicaid program, yet not enough to be eligible for premium tax credits under marketplace plans.

The states that have not expanded Medicaid are largely concentrated in the southern region of the United States.

Under the ACA, Medicaid eligibility was expanded for adults with incomes up to 138 percent of the federal poverty level (FPL). This expansion was originally written into the ACA as a requirement for all states, but due to a 2012 Supreme Court ruling in National Federation of Independent Business v. Sebelius, it is now just an option for states. To date, thirty-seven states (including the District of Columbia) have expanded Medicaid, either through traditional means or the Section 1115 waiver process. The states that have not expanded Medicaid are largely concentrated in the southern region of the United States. (See Map 1.)

In the South, African Americans are disproportionately represented. According to the U.S. Department of Health and Human Services Office of Minority Health, 58 percent of the African American population lived in the South as of 2017. They are also more likely to be uninsured, with Texas, Florida, and Georgia being home to the largest shares of uninsured African Americans. Some states have also proposed draconian work requirements as a condition for the participation in the Medicaid program. These requirements can only serve to stigmatize enrollees, deny coverage, and discourage low-income people from the support they desperately need. In Arkansas—one of nine states to date with 1115 waivers approved by the Trump administration allowing fully implemented work requirements—18,000 low-income people lost health care coverage as a result. This coverage loss comes as no surprise, because the use of work requirements for other safety-net programs, including Temporary Assistance for Needy Families (TANF), has proven them to be ineffective in their stated goal—promoting employment—yet highly effective in reducing program eligibility. Medicaid work requirements for three states have been struck down by the courts. Due to the failure to expand Medicaid, the South is now home to the nation's sickest people and is where health disparities between whites and people of color are the most pronounced.

Disparities in Health Outcomes

Increases in health insurance coverage under the ACA have improved access to medical care and have been linked to better outcomes for African Americans, such as earlier diagnosis and treatment of certain cancers. However, disparities still exist across health conditions when comparing African Americans and whites, including maternal mortality, infant mortality, heart disease, diabetes, cancer, and other health issues. Social factors, including economic disadvantage, inequities in education, and lack of access to health care, impact a person's ability to lead a healthy and productive life. For people in American society that experience racism and inequality in their daily lives, and throughout the lifespan, the impact of social factors on health are the gravest. Even with improved access to medical care under the ACA, the disparities in health outcomes between African Americans and whites are stark. African-American women are three times more likely to die of pregnancy-related causes than white women (see Figure 1).25 The African-American infant mortality rate is twice the rate for white infants (see Figure 2).26 African Americans are more likely to die from cancer and heart disease than whites, and are at greater risk for the onset of diabetes.27 However, death rates for African Americans with cancer and heart disease did drop over a fifteen year period.28 Across many chronic illnesses, however, African Americans are still more likely to die compared to other racial and ethnic groups. Homicides are also a leading cause of death for African Americans. In fact, African American children are ten times more likely to die by gun violence than white children (see Figure 3).

Health Care Provider Shortages

Dr. Jamila K. Taylor in "Racism, Inequality, and Health Care for African Americans"

Due to residential segregation, majority African American and Hispanic areas are more likely to lack hospitals and other health care providers. Therefore, place matters. When health care providers are located within majority African-American and Hispanic neighborhoods, they tend to offer lower-quality care.31 Often, people of color find themselves relying heavily on community health centers, emergency rooms or outpatient care, and community-based providers due to the lack of available primary care and mental health providers in a given geographic area. Traveling outside of the immediate geographic area to access health care may be an option for some people, yet this can be a challenge due to lack of access to transportation for those with limited incomes or for those living in rural areas. It is not difficult to locate where—and for whom—provider shortages are a serious concern. The Health Resources and Services Administration (HRSA) defines Health Professional Shortage Areas (HPSAs) as geographic, population, or facility-based designations that are indicative of health care provider shortages. Designations are made by the following health disciplines: primary care, dental health, and mental health. Federal regulations dictate the threshold for shortages by calculating the ratio of population to provider in order to identify high need areas. In 2018, there were 17,657 geographic areas, populations, and facilities identified by HRSA as not having enough health care providers. Mental health and primary care were the disciplines in the shortest supply. Medically Underserved Areas and Populations

(MUA/Ps) are another designation by HRSA. They are geographic areas and populations that lack adequate access to primary care providers. MUA/Ps identify specific populations that are likely to experience barriers to health care including the homeless, low-income people, people eligible for Medicaid, Native Americans, and migrant farmworkers. Designations are made by calculating the population-to-provider ratio, percent of population below the federal poverty level, percent of population over the age of 65, and the infant mortality rate.

Important Considerations for Health Care Specific to African Americans

Certain social factors, also referred to as social determinants of health, have important implications for health risk and the ability to attain health insurance coverage. Poverty, income inequality, wealth inequality, food insecurity, and the lack of safe, affordable housing are just a few. Another important social factor leading to poor health outcomes and economic disadvantage among African Americans is racism, because not only is it a stressor, but it impacts who gets what in America, particularly health care.

Racism's Wear and Tear on African Americans

African Americans have endured racism within American society for hundreds of years. Studies conducted over time have been consistent in proving that racism not only impacts social stratification, but also the ability of African Americans to be healthy—both mentally and physically. This burden—a burden that is indeed inescapable for black and brown people in this country—causes African Americans to die prematurely and experience chronic illnesses and mental health challenges at higher rates than white Americans. According to a study published in the journal of Psych neuroendocrinology, racist experiences bring on an increase in inflammation in African Americans. This increase in inflammation raises the risk of becoming chronically ill. The researchers of the study assert that, because the body's response to stressors—such as the adversity of racism—results in compromising systems that are critical in fending off disease, exposure to racism over long periods of time caused the health of African Americans to suffer greatly with chronic illness as the body's defenses were down due to inflammation. Chronic illnesses associated with experiencing racism include heart attack, neurodegenerative disease, and metastatic cancer. The study participants had similar socioeconomic backgrounds, which eliminated poverty as a stressor—a social factor that has also been linked to the onset of illness. Similar findings were yielded in some of the earliest studies looking at the impact of racism on the health of African Americans by University of Michigan public health researcher Arline Geronimous. After looking at biological factors associated with exposure to stressors, Geronimous hypothesized, in what is also referred to as the weathering hypothesis, that African Americans experienced health deterioration because of those stressors. Geronimous examined the allostatic load scores—that is, the cumulative wear and tear on the body's system brought on by the repeated adaptation to stressors—for adults aged 18–64. African Americans were found to have higher scores Americans. Once again, poverty was ruled out as a factor, due to the fact that the higher allostatic loads existed among African Americans of various socioeconomic backgrounds. Geronimous concluded that racism, and the burden of coping with it across the lifespan, leads to differences in health among African Americans and white Americans—including the onset of chronic illness and premature death. In addition to instigating poor health outcomes among African Americans, racism also creates barriers to economic opportunity and uneven access to health care. Even the health care system itself perpetuates racism and bias toward African Americans. This has been well documented with examples, including differences in pain management and treatment of African Americans when compared to whites experiencing the same health conditions, use of African Americans' bodies in medical experimentation, and racial bias in health algorithms for the purpose of guiding health decisions and assessing health care costs. Actions like these have led to a general distrust of the health care system within the African American community. Racism cannot be divorced from the other social factors outlined in this report, which give reason to the fact that African Americans are disproportionately affected by them.

Poverty

Across economic indicators, vast disparities exist between African Americans and whites that mirror the proportions seen in health disparities. Due to structural barriers, African Americans are more likely to be poor than white Americans and are less likely to have a full-time worker in the household. The poverty rate among African Americans was 20.8 percent in 2018, higher than for any other racial or ethnic group in the United States, and more than twice the poverty rate of white Americans. Growing up in poverty is also associated with toxic stress, of which the impact can reach crisis levels when a person is also grappling with the toxic stress brought on by racism. When African Americans are able to attain work, they are more likely to work in low-paying jobs that lack important benefits, including health insurance and paid leave. The African American poverty rate also shows how critical public programs such as Medicaid are to be helping ensure access to health care for this population. Because of these factors, Medicaid expansion helps more African Americans gain coverage than any other group.

Household Income Inequality

African American households have significantly lower household income than white households. The average household income for African Americans in 2018 was $41,361, while it was $70,642 for white households.50 (See Figure 4.) African Americans tend to make less than whites for the same jobs, pointing to unequal pay as a contributing factor in the gap in household income. Even when considering similar education levels, workers of color are consistently paid less than white workers. Income is a major factor in a family's ability to access health care, which can make up a significant share of household spending in terms of insurance premium costs and out-of-pocket costs. than whites.

The Wealth Gap

When it comes to accumulating wealth, the numbers are even more grim—white families now have approximately ten times the wealth of African American families, on average Research shows that the wealth gap impacts African Americans across the income and education spectrum, making it harder for them to own homes or build retirement savings. And while African Americans on average have less total debt than whites, the wealth gap means they are more likely to have costly, high-interest debt obligations. High health care costs and surprise medical bills can negatively affect an African American family's ability to reduce or eliminate debt, and ultimately the ability to create wealth—which could impact a family for generations.

Food Insecurity

Food insecurity is also an issue affecting many African Americans and has important implications for health outcomes and economic well-being. Food insecurity occurs when a household or family lacks access to adequate nutritious food. This happens due to the lack of financial means to purchase healthy food or by living in impoverished geographic areas void of grocery stores with whole, fresh foods. Neighborhoods that lack access to nutritious foods are also referred to as food deserts. The ten U.S. counties with the highest food insecurity rates are all at least 60 percent African American. African Americans experience hunger at twice the rate of white Americans, including one in four African American children.58 Hunger can also lead to chronic illness and has been associated with low-birth weight, diabetes, cancer, pregnancy complications, and mental distress.

The Lack of Safe and Affordable Housing

Housing and neighborhood safety are also important economic indicators that can impact health. Unfortunately, far too many African Americans have to grapple with neighborhood violence and environmental factors (such as a lack of clean water, exposure to lead paint, and pollution) that can negatively impact both their mental and physical health. Additionally, a relative lack of affordable housing options and home ownership continues to plague the African American community, largely due to longstanding racist practices such as redlining and subprime mortgages. The lack of affordable housing puts a financial strain on families and can pull resources away from necessities like food and medical care. For homeless and transient communities, it can be almost impossible to access health care or maintain adequate health regimens. Despite comprising just 13.4 percent of the total U.S. population, African Americans make up 40 percent of the homeless population, and are an overrepresented part of this group in every state.

Food Insecurity

Food insecurity is also an issue affecting many African Americans and has important implications for health outcomes and economic well-being. Food insecurity occurs when a household or family lacks access to adequate nutritious food. This happens due to the lack of financial means to purchase healthy food or by living in impoverished geographic areas void of grocery stores with whole, fresh foods. Neighborhoods that lack access to nutritious foods are also referred to as food deserts. The ten U.S. counties with the highest food insecurity rates are all at least 60 percent African American. African Americans experience hunger at twice the rate of white Americans, including one in four African American children. Hunger can also lead to chronic illness and has been associated with low-birth weight, diabetes, cancer, pregnancy complications, and mental distress.

The Lack of Safe and Affordable Housing

Housing and neighborhood safety are also important economic indicators that can impact health. Unfortunately, far too many African Americans have to grapple with neighborhood violence and environmental factors (such as a lack of clean water, exposure to lead paint, and pollution) that can negatively impact both their mental and physical health. Additionally, a relative lack of affordable housing options and home ownership continues to plague the African American community, largely due to longstanding racist practices such as redlining and subprime mortgages. The lack of affordable housing puts a financial strain on families and can pull resources away from necessities like food and medical care. For homeless and transient communities, it can be almost impossible to access health care or maintain adequate health regimens. Despite comprising just 13.4 percent of the total U.S. population, African Americans make up 40 percent of the homeless population, and are an overrepresented part of this group in every state Overview of Health Care Reform Plans Several health care reform proposals62 have been introduced by members of U.S. Congress and by 2020 presidential candidates. In this section, the most widely known and promising plans that have gained traction and media coverage in recent months are highlighted.63

Medicare for All

Medicare for All is a signature single-payer plan originally authored by Senator Bernie Sanders, setting forth a vision for major structural change of the health insurance system. It has since been endorsed and supported by Representative Pramila Jayapal (who introduced the House version of the legislation), Representative Alexandria Ocasio-Cortez, Senator Elizabeth Warren, Senator Kamala Harris, Senator Cory Booker, and a host of other progressive policymakers.64 It calls for a single federal program with comprehensive benefits for all U.S. residents that would replace all private insurance, Medicaid, Medicare, and the Children's Health Insurance Program (CHIP). The plan would be financed by taxes and eliminate premiums and cost-sharing or out-of-pocket costs, leading to major cost-savings for consumers in the long run. Considering the vast economic challenges for African Americans, savings in health care costs could help lead to better economic outcomes. In turn, health outcomes could also improve due to more comprehensive coverage available to all. Comprehensive health benefits under Medicare for All include medically necessary services in thirteen benefit categories, including home and community-based long-term care, dental care, hearing, vision care, comprehensive reproductive health care (including abortion services), and transportation to health care appointments for people with disabilities and low-income people.65 Drug prices would be negotiated annually and a formulary would be established. Medicare for All would also prohibit balance billing, also known as surprise billing, which happens when health providers bill patients for the difference in the total cost of a health care service and the amount paid by an insurer.66

Public Insurance Option

Public option plans call for a federal insurance option. These plans essentially build upon the ACA by adding a new option available to those seeking coverage. Former vice president Joe Biden has been an advocate for this plan and has included it in his platform as a 2020 presidential candidate. There are several versions of the public option—some that would leave the marketplace subsidy structure unchanged, and others that would enhance it for all plan participants. Some public option proposals even go so far as to eliminate individual health insurance plans created by the ACA. A key difference in the Biden plan, when compared with Medicare for All, is that it retains current public and private insurance sources. For people who like or prefer their private insurance, they can maintain it under the Biden plan. The Biden plan would retain major components of the ACA including protections for people with pre-existing conditions, premium subsidies, and Medicaid expansion, along with offering public insurance as an option to anyone who wants it.67 A public insurance option was initially part of the ACA as introduced in Congress but was taken out of the legislation later in the negotiations process. Biden's public option plan also aims to reduce the cost of prescription drugs by allowing importation of them from other countries, empowering Medicare to negotiate drug prices, and supporting the development of generic drugs.68 It would also offer tax credits to middle class families to help lower the cost of health insurance and eliminate the 400 percent federal poverty level income cap. The plan would eliminate balanced billing and be financed through capital gains taxes on rich individuals. Biden's plan also includes protecting access to contraception and abortion rights, as well as the promise to adopt California's strategy of public–private partnerships nationwide in addressing the U.S. maternal mortality crisis as major steps in building upon the ACA. Various versions of public insurance option legislation have also been introduced in Congress by Senator Ben Cardin, Representative Cedric Richmond, Senator Tim Kaine, Representative Jan Schakowsky, and others. Sixty-one percent of white respondents in a November 2019 Gallup poll prefer the private health insurance system, whereas 57 percent of nonwhite respondents prefer government-run insurance.69 The cost of health care is still of major concern for those people with private health insurance, more so than for those with public insurance sources.70

Ensuring Health Care Access and Affordable Coverage for African Americans

The single payer and public option insurance plans outlined in this report were developed in a way to help fill coverage gaps and get as many people insured as possible. The plans aim to do this by emphasizing affordability—addressing the high cost of insurance premiums and limiting out-of-pocket costs, including surprise medical bills, prescription drugs, and fees for direct health care services. Unfortunately, current health reform plans fall short in adequately addressing racism in the health care system. This stands in the way of ensuring health equity, namely full insurance coverage and quality health care access for African Americans. Cost to the individual is certainly an important factor in the conversation about health coverage and ensuring that people can access the health care services they need. However, in order for African Americans to attain meaningful insurance coverage and access to quality health care, the health care system must be transformed to better address the unique social factors that cause African Americans to remain in the coverage gap and how racism plays a role in their health outcomes. Furthermore, the economic challenges African Americans face serve as barriers to sustaining comprehensive coverage which can lead to poor health outcomes. It is simply not enough for insurance coverage to be affordable or even "free"—it must also serve as a tool in progress toward systemic change and equity that will help African Americans get ahead. To do this, getting to universal health care coverage will require that the following steps be taken:

Promote health equity by adequately addressing

racism, bias, discrimination, and other systemic barriers within the health care system. To do this, policymakers must acknowledge the historical foundations of racism and ensure that health care providers, personnel and staff are substantively trained to recognize and eliminate all forms of bias in the health care system. Accountability measures at both the individual and systems levels should be in place, including measures that link payment, professional certification, and licensure to quality of care. Incorporate evidence-based tools to adequately address health disparities that focus on quality of care that extend beyond health insurance coverage, including the impact of racism on the health of African Americans throughout the life course. In health reform efforts, policymakers must consider the social determinants and address how they impact health by working across sectors, including social support agencies and community-based providers with patient-centered approaches to care. Racist practices, such as those in the treatment and pain management of African Americans, should be eliminated. Protect and expanding access to insurance coverage and comprehensive benefits and bolstering the ACA benefit provisions and nondiscrimination guarantees. These efforts should include preserving coverage for people with pre-existing conditions by further codifying protections that ensure benefit inclusion and design decisions that do not result in limiting access to care. Policymakers should also build on the essential health benefits package to include important health care services currently omitted, such as long-term care and dental care. Protect the integrity of Medicaid, an important health insurance source for African Americans, by denying state efforts to impose draconian stipulations on coverage for enrollees such as work requirements. In order to close the coverage gap among African Americans, policymakers must also implement targeted strategies to incentivize and ensure Medicaid expansion in all southern states. Ensure access to quality providers and addressing provider shortages and hospital closures by anticipating increases in demand and working with HRSA to implement concrete strategies to close gaps in health care access for medically underserved areas/populations and health professional shortage areas. Strategies should include plans to not only increase the health care workforce, but also diversify it and offer technical support and training to minority-serving hospitals. Support the development of a robust, diverse, and culturally competent health care workforce by encouraging and facilitating diversity throughout the health care system and care teams, and adequately training all staff to be culturally sensitive. Payment rates and coverage guidelines for health care coverage should be developed in a way that supports fair, living wages and pay equity in the health care professions and jobs. Limit the cost of premiums and out-of-pocket costs, helping to make health insurance more affordable for individuals and families across the income spectrum. This should include limiting deductibles, prescription drug costs and other point-of-service charges, and completely eliminating surprise medical bills. All of these costs are major barriers to health care access, particularly for individuals and families with limited incomes. Strengthen access to trusted community-based providers currently available through safety-net programs, such as Medicaid, Medicare, and the Children's Health Insurance Program (CHIP). These programs are often lifelines for marginalized communities and they disproportionately serve people of color. Policymakers should develop health reform plans that are intentional in ensuring continued access to these vital sources of care, as well as seamless coordination with health insurance payers for people with coverage seeking care from community-based providers.

Chapter 7 References

1. "Quick Facts," U.S. Census Bureau, accessed November 15, 2019, https://www.census.gov/quickfacts/fact/table/US#.

Janel Jones, John Schmitt, and Valerie Wilson, "50 Years After The Kerner Commission, African Americans Are Better Off In Many Ways, But Are Still Disadvantaged By Racial Inequality," Economic Policy Institute, February 26, 2018, https://www.epi.org/publication/50-years-after-the-kerner-commission/.

2. Ibid.

Bowen Garret and Anju Gangopadhyaya, "Who Gained Health Insurance Coverage Under the ACA, and Where Do They Live?" Urban Institute and Robert Wood Johnson Foundation, December 2016, https://www.urban.org/sites/default/filespublication/86761/2001041-who-gained-health-insurance-coverage-under-the-aca-and-where-do-they-live.pdf.

"Health Insurance Coverage in the United States: 2018," U.S. Census Bureau, November 2019, https://www.census.gov/content/dam/Census/library/publications/2019/demo/p60-267.pdf.

3 Ibid. "The Real Cost of Health Care: Interactive Calculator Estimates Both Direct and Hidden Household Spending," Henry J. Kaiser Family Foundation, February 21, 2019, https://www.kff.org/health-costs/press-release/interactive-calculator-estimates-both-direct-and-hidden-household-spending/.

4. Calculated by the author using the average annual household income for African Americans ($41,361) and the annual health care premium cost for families ($8,200).

5U.S. Census Bureau, "Health Insurance Coverage in The United States."

5. "Key Facts About the Uninsured Population," Henry J. Kaiser Family Foundation, December 7, 2018, https://www.kff.org/uninsured/fact-sheet/key-facts-about-the-uninsured-population/.

6. Sara R. Collins, Herman K. Bhupal, and Michelle M. Doty, "Health Insurance Coverage Eight Years After The ACA: Fewer Uninsured Americans and Shorter Coverage Gaps," The Commonwealth Fund, February 7, 2019, https://www.commonwealthfund.org/publications/issue-briefs/2019/feb/health-insurance-coverage-eight-years-after-aca.

7. "Program History: Medicaid," Centers for Medicare and Medicaid Services, accessed November 16, 2019, https://www.medicaid.gov/about-us/program-history/index.html.

8. "Medicaid and Medicare Are Important to African Americans," National Committee to Preserve Social Security and Medicare, January 28, 2019, https://www.ncpssm.org/documents/medicare-policy-papers/medicare-medicaid-important-african-americans/.

9. Rachel Garfield, Kendal Orgera, and Anthony Damico, "The Coverage Gap: Uninsured Poor Adults in States that Do Not Expand Medicaid," Henry J. Kaiser Family Foundation, March 21, 2019, https://www.kff.org/medicaid/issue-brief/the-coverage-gap-uninsured-poor-adults-in-states-that-do-not-expand-medicaid/.

10. "Overview of the Affordable Care Act and Medicaid," Medicaid and CHIP Payment and Access Commission, accessed November 17, 2019, https://www.macpac.gov/subtopic/overview-of-the-affordable-care-act-and-medicaid/.

11. *National Federation of Independent Business v. Sebelius*, 567 U.S. 519 (2012).

Section 1115 Medicaid demonstration waivers allow states to test new approaches in Medicaid that differ from what is required by federal statute. "Medicaid Expansion to the New Adult Group," Medicaid and CHIP Payment and Access Commission, accessed November 17, 2019, https://www.macpac.gov/subtopic/medicaid-expansion/.

12. "Profile: African Americans."

Peggy Bailey, Matt Broaduss, Shelby Gonzales, and Kyle Hayes, "African American Uninsured Rate Dropped by More Than a Third Under the Affordable Care Act: Repealing ACA and Cutting Medicaid Would Undercut Progress," Center on Budget and Policy Priorities, June 1, 2017, https://www.cbpp.org/research/health/african-american-uninsured-rate-dropped-by-more-than-a-third-under-affordable-care.

13. "State Proposals for Medicaid Work and Community Engagement Requirements," National Academy for State Health Policy, accessed November 19, 2019, https://nashp.org/wp-content/uploads/2018/01/Medicaid-Work-Requirements-Chart_10_31_19_Final.pdf.

14. Phil Galewitz, "Study: Arkansas Medicaid Work Requirement Hits Those Already Employed," *Kaiser Health News*, June 19, 2019, https://khn.org/news/study-arkansas-medicaid-work-requirements-hit-those-already-employed/.

15. Judith Solomon, "Medicaid Work Requirements Can't Be Fixed: Unintended Consequences Are Inevitable Result," Center on Budget and Policy Priorities, January 10, 2019, https://www.cbpp.org/research/health/medicaid-work-requirements-cant-be-fixed.

16. "America's Health Rankings: 2018 Annual Report," United Health Foundation, https://www.americashealthrankings.org/learn/reports/2018-annual-report/findings-state-rankings; "Rural Health Disparities," Rural Health Information Hub, accessed November 17, 2019, https://www.ruralhealthinfo.org/topics/rural-health-disparities.

17. Laurie McGinley, "ACA Linked to Reduce Racial Disparities, Earlier Diagnosis and Treatment in Cancer Care: New Research

Backs Up Earlier Data Showing the Law Increased Access to Care," *Washington Post*, June 2, 2019, https://www.washingtonpost.com/health/2019/06/02/aca-linked-reduced-racial-disparities-earlier-diagnosis-treatment-cancer-care/.

18. Emily E. Peterson, Nicole L. Davis, David Goodman, Shannon Cox, and others, "Racial/Ethnic Disparities in Pregnancy-Related Deaths—United States 2007–2016," Centers for Disease Control and Prevention, September 6, 2019, https://www.cdc.gov/mmwr/volumes/68/wr/mm6835a3.htm?s_cid=mm6835a3_w.

19. "Infant Health Mortality and African Americans," U.S. Department of Health and Human Services Office of Minority Health, accessed November 17, 2019, https://minorityhealth.hhs.gov/omh/browse.aspx?lvl=4&lvlid=23.

20. "African American Death Rate Drops 25 Percent," Centers for Disease Control and Prevention, May 2, 2017, https://www.cdc.gov/media/releases/2017/p0502-aa-health.html.

21. Ibid.

Yolanda T. Mitchell and Tiffany L. Bromfield, "Gun Violence and the Minority Experience," National Council on Family Relations, January 10, 2019,

22. "The Impact of Poverty." P. Braveman, M. Dekker, S. Egerter, T. Sadegh-Nobari, and C. Pollack, "How Does Housing Affect Health: An Examination of the Many Ways Housing Can Influence Health and Strategies To Improve Health Through Emphasis on Healthier Homes," Robert Wood Johnson Foundation, May 1, 2011, https://www.rwjf.org/en/library/research/2011/05/housing-and-health.html.

23. Joy Moses, "Demographic Data Project: Race, Ethnicity, and Homelessness," National Alliance to End Homelessness—Homelessness Research Institute, accessed November 17, 2019,

https://endhomelessness.org/wp-content/uploads/2019/07/3rd-Demo-Brief-Race.pdf.

24. Jeanne Lambrew and Jennifer MIshory, "Comparison of Health Reform Legislation Creating Public Plans," The Century Foundation, August 7, 2019, https://tcf.org/content/commentary/comparison-health-reform-legislation-creating-public-plans/.

25. Luna Lopes, Liz Hamel, Audrey Kearny, and Mollyann Brodie, "KFF Health Tracking Poll—October 2019: Health Care in the Democratic Debates, Congress, and the Courts," Henry J. Kaiser Family Foundation, October 15, 2019, https://www.kff.org/health-reform/poll-finding/kff-health-tracking-poll-october-2019/.

26. H.R. 1384, Medicare for All, accessed November 18, 2019, https://www.congress.gov/116/bills/hr1384/BILLS-116hr1384ih.pdf.

27. Ibid.

"Balanced Billing," U.S. Centers for Medicare and Medicaid Services—HealthCare.gov, accessed November 17, 2019, https://www.healthcare.gov/glossary/balance-billing/.

Dan Diamond, "Biden Unveils Health Care Plan: Affordable Care Act 2.0," Politico, July 15, 2019, https://www.politico.com/story/2019/07/15/joe-biden-health-care-plan-1415850.

28. Ibid., and "Health Care," Joe Biden For President, accessed November 18, 2019, https://joebiden.com/healthcare/.

29. Gallup News poll conducted November 1–14, 2019, available for download from https://news.gallup.com/file/poll/268988/191204GovtResponsibility.pdf.

30. Tami Luhby, "Americans are still pretty happy with their private health insurance," CNN, December 9, 2019, https://www.cnn.com/2019/12/09/politics/gallup-private-health-insurance-satisfaction/index.html.

31. For additional recommendations, please see Jamila Taylor and Jen Mishory, "Health Reform's North Star: 10 Guidelines to Reach Universal Health Care Coverage," The Century Foundation, November 13, 2019, https://tcf.org/content/commentary/health-reforms-north-star-10-guidelines-reach-universal-health-care-coverage/.

8

Types of Depression

Depression

You have probably come across people using the word "depressed" to describe someone with mere sadness or the normal, everyday blues that last only a couple of days and get better on their own. But that's just wrong. Depression is a serious mental health condition accompanied by feelings of extreme despondency that can result in a reduction in a person's vitality, vigor, or spirits. Depression affects a person both biologically and psychologically. And as per the American Psychiatric Association's Diagnostic and Statistical Manual of Mental Disorders, Fifth Edition (DSM-V), one can say he or she is depressed when they see at least five of the following signs for more than two weeks nearly every day. Depressed mood or irritable most of the day. Loss of interest or pleasure in most activities, most of each day. A significant change in weight (5 percent) or in appetite.

Change in sleep: Either not being able to sleep (Insomnia) or not being able to wake up (hypersomnia).

Change in activity: Psychomotor agitation or retardation Fatigue or loss of energy.

Guilt/worthlessness: Feelings of worthlessness or excessive or inappropriate guilt. Concentration: Losing ability to think or concentrate, or more indecisiveness.

Suicidality: Thoughts of death or suicide or has suicide plan. Here are 10 depression facts. Some of these can be interesting, yet common symptoms include sadness, tiredness, trouble focusing or concentrating unhappiness anger irritability frustration loss of interest in pleasurable or fun activities sleep issues (too much or too little) no energy craving unhealthy foods anxiety isolation, persistent feeling of sadness and loss of interest.

Did you know: Depression Doesn't Always Have a "Good" Reason (verywellmind.com).

Stress Level Test (Self-Assessment), www.psycom.net/stress-test

Am I too stressed? How much stress is too much? Use this short quiz to measure whether your stress level is too high.

Answer the quiz questions above is the website to see if you or a loved one may be suffering from too much stress.

Instructions: A list of questions that relate to life experiences common among people who are experiencing heavy stress. Please read each question carefully and indicate how often you have experienced the same or similar challenges in the past few months.

Do I Have Test Anxiety? (Self-Assessment), www.psycom.net/test-anxiety-quiz-assessment/

A little nervousness before a test or exam is normal, but if you experience extreme stress and anxiousness that interfere with your ability to complete the test, you may be suffering from test anxiety

Answer the quiz questions website above to see if you or a loved one may be suffering from test anxiety. Instructions: Below is a list of questions that relate to life experiences common among people who struggle with test anxiety. Please read each question carefully and indicate how often you have experienced the same or similar challenges in the past few months.

Does My Partner Have Depression? (Self-Assessment Test

https://www.psycom.net/does-my-partner-have-depression

Are you worried that your husband/boyfriend or wife/girlfriend may be depressed? Take this short quiz to see if your spouse is experiencing symptoms common among people with depression.

Answer the quiz questions website above to see if your partner may have depression. Instructions: Below is a list of questions that relate to life experiences common among people who have been diagnosed with depression. Please read each question carefully and indicate how often your partner has experienced the same or similar challenges in the past few months.

How to Convince Someone You Care About to Get Help for Depression

Katie Hurley, LCSW, Psycom.net

When you suspect someone, you care about is suffering from depression, your support and encouragement can go a long way in getting them on the road to recovery. Here's how you can help them to help themselves.

Signs Your Loved One is in a Bad Place Emotionally

First, know what symptoms you are looking for. Years back, well before I became a therapist, a close friend was clearly exhibiting signs of depression, but her husband and I didn't know what to look for; just that something was "off." We thought she'd snap back and soon be herself, but it took Ann saying she was going to down an entire bottle of sleeping pills for us to realize she was in serious trouble.

Be concerned if your loved one:

Feels hopeless, negative, cannot voice one positive aspect of life. Experiences persistent sadness or feelings of emptiness versus occasional low moods. Has difficulty sleeping or is constantly sleeping; is unable to eat or constantly eating. Has pronounced lack of energy and /or difficulty focusing. Is irritable. Shows no interest in previously enjoyable activities. Expresses a wish to be dead. Expresses a desire to kill him or herself. If your loved one is not only expressing suicidal thoughts but has also created a plan to commit suicide and/or is talking about giving away his or her belongings, you cannot delay. Immediate help is needed.

Call 911 or 1-800-SUICIDE or 1-800-273-TALK.

Do's and Don'ts

If the situation is not urgent then do not take away his or her autonomy. Rather, take these steps.

Timing is Important

Which is the best place to have a sensitive conversation with someone who is emotionally fragile?

At a crowded restaurant where the tables are jammed together and there is no privacy

When the two of you have privacy and no distractions (i.e., children underfoot), looming deadlines or appointments. Okay, the choices above were pretty exaggerated, but the point is clear. The two of you should be alone and fairly relaxed.

Be Empathetic, Not judgmental

Remember in Moonstruck when Cher said to a besotted Nicolas Cage, "Snap out of it." Well, a depressed person needs to have his or her feelings validated, not belittled, or otherwise called into question. Be gentle and use "I" statements – such as "I love you very much. You are a very special person to me, and I am concerned that everything is not okay." It is quite possible your loved one will react defensively, so work hard to not get offended but to stay loving and supportive. Say something like, "I think you are one of the kindest, smartest, loyal people I know and it feels like you are going through

a rough patch and I'd like to help you the way you would help me."
Show Your Knowledge About Depression

A depressed person may not be aware he or she is ill – and that the illness likely is treatable. It can be helpful to share a symptom list of depression so that your loved one can recognize what is going on. You might say something like, "Some of the things that are concerning to me is that you haven't gone to the gym in over a month, and you usually go three times a week." If you have personal positive experience with therapy, you can bring that up, or start a conversation about the unfortunate stigma around mental health and going to therapy.

Offer to Do Legwork

The task of finding a therapist can feel overwhelming even without being crippled by the paralysis of depression. You can do some research to find a few potential therapists and offer to accompany your loved one to the first session. You can use an online directory to find a therapist based on your location, insurance, and language, and can see which conditions each mental health professional specializes in.

If money is an issue (it is certainly often used as an excuse), if possible, you can offer to pay for the therapy or to help your loved one find an affordable therapist. A lot of therapists offer a sliding scale, which means that they will charge you a fee that works for you. Some therapists even take on a number of clients for free as part of an ethics code that says they will provide some services pro bono as a gesture of good will.

Be Patient

Keep in mind that finding the right therapist can often take time and that it's fine to meet with several different mental health professionals until your loved one feels like they can connect with that person. Don't be afraid to ask for complimentary consultations by phone or by Skype as you are going through this process, as some therapists will spend half an hour on the phone with you for free. A hard as it is to see someone you care deeply about suffer, unless the person is in serious danger of self-harm all you can do is be encouraging and let him or her know your love and support are unconditional, and you will be there every step of the way.

Article by Sherry Amatenstein, LCSW, Psycom.net

According to the National Institute of Mental Health depression is one of the most commonly diagnosed mental disorders in the United States and can be attributed to a combination of genetic, biological, environmental, and psychological factors. If you have a friend or family member struggling with depression, you might not know what to say or how to lend support. The single best thing you can do for a friend with depression is listen without judgment. There are a number of phrases that are sometimes used with good intentions but can actually make a person with depression feel worse. Avoid these phrases when supporting a friend with depression:

"Don't think about it"

Some people with depression actually suffer from rumination. Ruminating means repetitively going over a thought or problem without completion, and it can contribute to increased feelings of worthlessness or helplessness in depressed patients.

A person can't simply depression away and telling a person to stop thinking about their problems can actually trigger them to engage in rumination. One study found that although ruminators do tend to reach out for help, they often don't get the support they seek, and their rumination causes social friction. When a support system pulls away or tells the depressed person to stop thinking about it, the ruminator has more to ruminate about.3

"Think positive!"

Although psychotherapists often use cognitive reframing to help depressed patients replace negative thoughts with positive ones, this process takes time and helps the patient explore the roots of the negative thought cycle. Telling a depressed person to "think positive" is dismissive of the medical condition that causes the symptoms and places blame on the person struggling with the disease.

"I know how you feel"

Although this statement is empathic and meant to help the depressed person feel understood, it can backfire. There is a significant difference between clinical depression and sadness. It's normal to experience feelings of sadness, but depression is a mood disorder that negatively impacts a person's ability to attend to normal daily activities.

Statements like this one minimize the person's pain.

"Count your blessings"

There tends to be a lot of guilt and shame with depression. Depressed people often describe feelings of guilt, worthlessness, and helplessness. Because depression is an invisible disease (people don't necessary appear "depressed"), there is a stigma surrounding the disease. Statements like "count your blessings" or "be grateful for what you have" imply that the person is depressed because he or she simply can't see what they do have.

"It could be worse"

Comparisons to other people fighting other battles are rarely useful. When a depressed person reaches out for social support, he or she is looking for empathy and compassion.

Although there might be other people suffering from any number of medical conditions, telling a depressed person that someone else has it worse only makes that person feel ashamed.

"Get over it"

Depression is a serious medical condition, and simply telling someone to move on or get over it won't actually cure it. This kind of statement lacks compassion and will likely make the person with depression feel shamed and misunderstood. There are no perfect answers when it comes to supporting a friend or loved one with depression, and questions can be just as helpful as statements when a depressed person opens up. Try a few of these empathic responses: How can I help you during this difficult time? I'm sorry that you're hurting. I'm here for you. Tell me more about it. Would you like to take a walk with me? Can I keep you company today? Can I bring you dinner this week? Thank you for sharing this with me so that I can understand what you're going through.

9

Black, Asian and Minority Ethnic (BAME) Communities

Mental Health Foundation, June 19, 2019,
https://www.mentalhealth.org.uk/a-to-z/b/
black-asian-and-minority-ethnic-bame-communities

It is important to note that BAME is a term that covers a wide range of people with a very diverse range of needs. Different ethnic groups have different experiences of mental health problems that reflect their culture and context. Data collected on mental health in minority ethnic groups can often be subject to small sample sizes, meaning our ability to look at mental health within a specific ethnic group is sometimes limited. For instance, there may be a small number of people from a certain ethnicity group taking part in a research survey. This means that there is much more we still need to know about ethnicity and mental health in the UK.

Racism and discrimination

People from BAME communities can experience racism in their personal lives, ranging from casual slights to explicit hurtful comments and verbal or physical aggression. Research suggests that experiencing racism can be very stressful and have a negative effect on overall health and mental health. There is a growing body of research to suggest that those exposed to racism may be more likely to experience mental health problems such as psychosis and depression.

Social and economic inequalities

BAME communities are also often faced with disadvantages in society. They are more likely to experience poverty, have poorer educational outcomes, higher unemployment, and contact with the criminal justice system, and may face challenges accessing or receiving appropriate professional services.8–9 For example: Among 16 to 24 year old, unemployment rates are highest for people from a Black background (26%) and from a Pakistani or Bangladeshi background (23%) in comparison with their White counterparts (11%). Even when employed, men and women from some ethnic groups are paid less on average than those from other groups with similar qualifications and experience. Pakistani and Bangladeshi communities consistently have high rates of poverty, as do Black, Chinese, and Other ethnic communities. Homelessness is a key issue among minority ethnic groups, with 37% of statutory homeless households from a 'BME background' in 2013. Each of these can act as risk factors for the development of mental health problems. Different communities understand and talk about mental health in different ways. In some communities, mental health problems are rarely spoken about and can be seen in a negative light.9 This can discourage people within the community from talking about their mental health and may be a barrier to engagement with health services.

Criminal justice system

There is growing concern over unmet mental health needs among BAME individuals within the criminal justice system, particularly in the youth justice system. On 2016 report on the youth justice system in England and Wales found over 40% of children are from BAME backgrounds, and more than one third have a diagnosed mental health problem. The level of need may be even greater than this as it has also been found that BAME individuals are less likely to have mental health problems or learning disabilities identified upon entry to the justice system.

Other factors

Many groups face inequalities in physical and mental health. This can be due to factors like disability, sexuality, gender, and age. In order to understand different BAME communities' experiences of mental health problems and of services provided it is also necessary to consider these other aspects in addition to race and ethnicity.

Mental health stigma

Different communities understand and talk about mental health in different ways. In some communities, mental health problems are rarely spoken about and can be seen in a negative light. This can discourage people within the community from talking about their mental health and may be a barrier to engagement with health services.

Different BAME groups and particular mental health concerns

Different BAME groups may be more likely to face particular mental health concerns. It is important to note, however, that our understanding of these mental health concerns is limited by the quality of the data collected.

Black / African / Caribbean / Black British people. The Adult Psychiatric Morbidity Survey (APMS) found that Black men were more likely than their White counterparts to experience a psychotic disorder in the last year. Risk of psychosis in Black Caribbean groups is estimated to be nearly seven times higher than in the White population. The impact of the higher rates of mental illness is that people from these groups are more likely than average to encounter mental health services. Detention rates under the Mental Health Act during 2017/18 were four times higher for people in the 'Black' or 'Black British' group than those in the 'White' group. The Count Me in Census, which collects information on inpatient care, found higher than average admission and detention rates for Black groups in every year since 2006 to 2010. Black men were reported to have the highest rates of drug use and drug dependency than other groups. Whilst the White Caucasian population experienced the highest rates for suicidal thoughts, suicide rates are higher among young men of Black African, Black Caribbean origin, and among middle aged Black African, Black Caribbean and South Asian women than among their White British counterparts.

Asian/ Asian British

This term refers to people in the UK from Indian, Pakistani, Bangladeshi, Chinese and any other Asian backgrounds. The latest APMS found no meaningful differences between Asian people and their White British counterparts in terms of experiencing psychotic disorders or common mental health problems. People of Indian and Pakistani origin showed higher levels of mental wellbeing than other ethnic groups as did those of African-Caribbean origin. Suicidal thoughts were less common in Asian people than White British people, as was the likelihood of self-harming behavior. Those identifying as Asian or Asian British are one-third less likely to be in contact with mental health or learning disability services. Within the South Asian community in England and Wales, research has indicated that older South Asian women seem to be an at-risk group for suicide. One 2018 review found that non-European immigrant women, including young South Asian women, were a high-risk group for suicide attempts. Findings from the last Count Me In census found that the number of people in the Asian or Asian British groups who spent time compulsorily detained in hospital rose by approximately 9% from 2005 to 2010.There are some studies that suggest prevalence of mental ill-health (both common mental health problems and psychotic illness) is lower among Chinese people than their White British counterparts. Chinese people are underrepresented in mental health services, rates of admission to mental health inpatient facilities in England and Wales were lower among the Chinese population compared to the national average. Further research is required to explore whether this is because the community experiences better mental health than the general population or if they experience specific barriers to accessing mental health services. It is important to note that these findings may not be reflective of true prevalence of mental health problems among Asian communities in the UK as the reasons explored above may mean that people in these communities are less likely to report that they are experiencing mental health problems. Other ethnic groups Irish people living in the UK have much higher hospital admission rates for mental health problems than other ethnic groups. They have higher rates of depression and alcohol problems and are at greater risk of suicide. Comhar men's groups. We are currently working on a project with Irish men in mid-life living in Camden. The project was developed following a piece of research in the London Boroughs of Camden and Islington that identified two particular risk factors for poor mental health and suicide: being a man in mid-life and being born in the Republic of Ireland. The self-management courses aim to equip participants with skills and learning that will mitigate that risk. Find out more Culturally appropriate treatment interventions. Research points to a strong need for greatly increased cultural competency in mental health services. This may include practical improvements in language (interpreting, translating, literacy support), meeting faith-related and religious needs, culturally appropriate food, gender-specific services and staff, increasing the ethnic diversity of staff, and action to address and reduce experiences of racism and discrimination. Refugees and asylum seekers. Refugees and asylum seekers may experience exclusion, marginalization, and inequalities of access to services. They are more likely to experience mental health problems than the general population, including higher rates of depression, PTSD, and other anxiety disorders. The increased vulnerability to mental health problems that refugees, and asylum seekers face is linked to pre-migration experiences (such as war trauma) and post-migration conditions (such as separation from family, difficulties with asylum procedures and poor housing).

Data shows that they are less likely to receive support than the general population.

Further Information and Resources

Local Mind – a useful way of finding out what is available in your area, such as specific BAME groups. They also have a useful information page that outlines their work in this area.

Black Thrive – an organization that aims to end the stigma associated with mental health and address mental health inequalities experienced by Lambeth's Black communities. Sharing Voices – a charity in Bradford that aims to reduce mental health and related inequalities for BAME communities.

The Chinese Mental Health Association – an organization that is involved in providing direct services, increasing mental health awareness, and representing Chinese mental health issues in public forums and raising its profile in the overall Chinese community.

10

Policing AmeriKKK in Black and Brown Communities

A history of traumatic experience from police arrests and brutality leads to PTSD. Walking while black, jogging while black, sleeping while black, gardening while black, biking while black, buying a home while black—what can't we do in America as a black person? Police brutality is damaging the black community's mental health! A history of traumatic experience due to police brutality during arrests leads to PTSD. This is a public health issue, and we, as black and brown Americans, suggest going a step further and incorporating a public health perspective into the twenty-first century. Using a public health perspective would mean more than the prosecution of a single police officer. Police brutality indicts an entire system of recruiting, hiring, training, and evaluating police officers. "To be a Negro in this country and to be relatively conscious is to be in a state of rage almost all the time," quoted James Baldwin. We are in mental distress and while we are strong, capable, and intelligent. We also need help so that, together, we can correct the wrongs in the system or perhaps replace the system itself. This is not new; it happens every day. Nowadays, one cannot do anything as a person of color; particularly, black people are targeted. Within the black community, we generally acknowledge and discuss the experiences of racism and the detrimental impact of racism on equitable access to resources, including education, housing health care, etc. We less frequently discuss the detrimental impact racism has on our mental health. It is important to emphasize that we, as black Americans, are not responsible for the existence or experience of racism, and we unfairly are burdened with the responsibility of coping with the painful existence of oppressive experiences.

Let us take a look history and the most recent real-life stories of black and brown Americans dying at the hands of police officers:

2019 – Officer Amber Guyger charged with manslaughter after entering an apartment she thought was hers as she says and killing an unarmed black man who lived there.

2018 – Botham Jeans's killing happened only days after another officer, Roy Oliver, was sentenced to only fifteen years for the murder of Jordan Edwards, a fifteen-year-old boy who was leaving a party with friends.

2018 – June 10, 2018, Antwon Rose Jr., a seventeen-year-old unarmed black male was killed in the Pittsburgh suburbs when he fled a car that had been stopped by police. He was shot in the back by Officer Michael Rosfeld, who had been hired one month before and had only been formally sworn in by hours before he took the teenager's life.

2019

Officer Amber Guyger–Charged with manslaughter after entering an apartment she thought was hers as she says and killing an unarmed black man who lived there

2018

Botham Jeans' killing happen only days after another officer Roy Oliver, was sentenced to only 15 years for the murder of Jordan Edwards– a 15-year-old boy who was leaving a party with friends.

2018

June 10, 2018 Antwon Rose Jr.– a 17-year-old unarmed black males, was killed in Pittsburgh suburbs as he fled a car that had been stopped by police. He was shot in the back by officer Michael Rosfeld who had been hired one month before and had only been formally sworn in by hours before he took the teenager life's life.

Two days after Rose's death, Boston University School of Health and the University of Pennsylvania released a study that found the high rate of unarmed African Americans being killed at the hands of the police has caused more incidents of depression, stress, and other mental health issues among black and brown people. In other words, overwhelming police brutality is damaging the mental health of black and brown folks at an alarming rate for even those who have no direct connection to the men, women, and teens who lost their lives to police brutality.

2020 – Breonna Taylor, a twenty-six-year-old emergency health worker was shot eight times in her home on March 13. She was asleep before the police battering ram entered her home and killing her. The disturbing part is that the police ram the wrong house while looking for a suspect who was already in custody. The whole time the fucking officer had the wrong address.

I guess all black people look alike!

2020 – Ahmaud Arbery, twenty-five, a black man was jogging in a neighborhood where he lived in Brunswick on February 23, 2020, when a white man and his son chased and shot him dead and later told the police that he looked like a suspect in a number of burglaries in the area.

2020 – George Floyd, forty-four, black. On May 25, 2020, George Floyd, an African American man, died in Powderhorn, a neighborhood south of downtown Minneapolis, Minnesota. While Floyd was handcuffed and lying face down on a city street during an arrest, Derek Chauvin, a white Minneapolis police officer, kept his knee on the right side of Floyd's neck for eight minutes and forty-six seconds. According to the criminal complaint against Chauvin, two minutes and fifty-three seconds of that time occurred after Floyd became unresponsive. Officers Tou Thao, J. Alexander Kueng, and Thomas K. Lane participated in Floyd's arrest with Kueng holding Floyd's back, Lane holding his legs, and Thao looking on as he stood nearby.

Enough is enough. I fear for all my black brothers and sisters around the world we can't do anything! (by the police, updated on May 2020).

My condolences to the families, friends, and loved ones of those who have been killed by police.

The Latest Police Shootings Database, May 16, 2020, https://killedbypolice.net/

380 People Have Been Shot and Killed by Police in 2020.

1004 People Have Been Shot and Killed by Police in 2019.

992 People Have Been Shot and Killed by Police in 2018.

986 People Have Been Shot and Killed by Police in 2017.

962 People Have Been Shot and Killed by Police in 2016.

994 People Have Been Shot and Killed by Police in 2015.

11

When Racism Takes Over Health Care in Black and Brown Communities

3 ways to help doctors and staff deal with racist patients

Joanne Finnegan, Fierce Health Care, June 14, 2017, https://www.fiercehealthcare.com/practices/3-ways-to-help-doctors-and-staff-deal-racist-patients

J. Corey Williams, M.D., a resident physician at Yale University Department of Psychiatry, will not soon forget the call he got from a nurse about a patient who was being loud, belligerent, and disruptive. The petite elderly Caucasian patient at the center of the disruption took one look at him and said, 'I don't want no nigger doctor," Williams recalled in an opinion piece for The Hill.

Lachelle Dawn Weeks, M.D., a resident in internal resident at Brigham and Women's Hospital in Boston, recalls the elderly white woman who insulted her with the advice to not "waste her affirmative action," in an opinion piece on STAT.

Physicians who are cultural and religious minorities can face the burden of discrimination. However, "particularly at a time when some Americans feel emboldened to speak and act in bigoted ways, clinicians need support managing patients who make derogatory and abusive remarks," Weeks writes.

On April 24, 2020, I broke my arm and was sent to an all-white orthopedic. I am always uncomfortable when I am the only colored person in the room. The front desk clerk knew I was the first person to be seen, but she asks me to leave the office go to the cafeteria and wait until someone calls me. That has never happened to me in my thirty-three years of living. It is a hurtful feeling to experience racism in the health care system. I will never be seen at an all-white clinic never again. I was seen for only two minutes.

Racism Is a Mental Illness in Black and Brown Communities

Is Racism a Mental Illness?

Shayla Love, *Vice News*, Vice.com, July 8, 2020, https://www.vice.com/en_ca/article/dyzd57/is-racism-a-mental-illness

On the *Oprah Winfrey Show* in 1992, Jane Elliott, the educator known for teaching students about prejudice by biasing them against blue or brown eyes, came to an incisive conclusion about racism. "What we're dealing with here is mental illness," she said. Members of the audience started clapping. "Racism is a mental illness. If you judge other people by the color of their skin, by the amount of a chemical in their skin, you have a mental problem. You are not dealing well with reality." This grainy television clip has been recirculating on social media due to the explosion of online advocacy from the current Black Lives Matter protests. Google searches for "racism is a mental illness" have spiked to a level unseen over the last 10 years, and on Twitter, many have declaratively shared the sentiment. The belief that someone isn't your equal because of the way they look must mean that person's brain isn't working correctly, these people are saying; they are ill.

But the comparison of racism to mental illness is a fraught one. Disability and mental health advocates push back strongly against the association, saying that racism is a choice, while mental disorders, like depression, anxiety, bipolar disorder, and schizophrenia are not. Calling racism, a mental illness perpetuates the stigma around mental illnesses, and continues the practice of using mental health language in a derogatory way. (Think calling situations or people you don't like "crazy" or "insane.") The impulse to attribute racist acts and hate crimes to mental illness also conflates mental illness and violence, even though most mentally ill people do not engage in violent acts and are at most risk of harming themselves, not to others.

The push to define racism as a mental illness is decades old, though, and originally came from mental health providers. In 1969, a group of prominent Black psychiatrists petitioned the American Psychiatric Association (APA) to add extreme bigotry to The Diagnostic and Statistical Manual of Mental Disorders, or DSM, the handbook of mental disorders, now in its 5th edition. Their petition was rejected.

The APA's reason for rejection reveals something about the underlying desire for racism to be designated as a sickness. For something to be considered a mental illness, it must deviate from typical thinking or behavior, and cause disruption and distress to a person's life. The APA said that racism was, in contrast, so widespread that it was a cultural issue, not a psychopathology. Racism is too common, in other words, to be an illness. Asking whether extreme racism is a mental illness often goes along with trying to understand extremely racist acts. How is anyone to make sense of white police officers tackling a 23-year-old Elijah McClain to the ground, putting him in a carotid hold, as he cried, vomited, said that he couldn't breathe, and pleaded to go to his home nearby? Or two white men in New Jersey, part of the All Lives Matter countermovement to Black Lives Matter, re-enacting George Floyd's death with one pinning the other to the ground under his knee as Black Lives Matter protesters marched by? Or the nooses hung in trees and in the garage stall of Bubba Wallace, the only Black driver in NASCAR, at the Talladega Superspeedway? By not calling racism a mental illness, does that mean we accept these acts of racism as normal human behavior? If racism is not a sickness, why is it so hard to get extremely racist people to change their minds? Doesn't their refusal mean that their beliefs are not opinions, but delusions? These are complex questions. Racism exists on a spectrum, from extreme racist beliefs and hate crimes to the prejudices all white people have and need to reckon with. Delusions involving race can also be a symptom of other psychotic disorders; their placement in the DSM is not up for debate.

When asking whether racism should be considered a mental illness, it's worth asking another question: Would framing racism as such help us fight racism? One of the reasons we have diagnostic categories for mental illness is so that we can try to treat those illnesses. If racism was thought of as a mental illness, would it help efforts to make the world a less racist place, or make them harder? In 1965, psychiatrist Alvin Poussaint went to Jackson, Mississippi to provide mental health treatment to civil rights workers and desegregate hospitals. While there, he said, he experienced the extreme racism that he would later try to have added to the DSM. "It was ever-present, and it was a kind of state of terror," he said. Even when talking to other doctors, trying to explain why hospitals should be desegregated, he encountered prejudice and bigotry. The white doctors would resist, saying they believed it was best if Black people remained segregated in the health care system and had separate facilities. "I felt it was like a mental disturbance, because you couldn't reason with people over it," Poussaint said. "I began to appreciate how deep it went, in terms of denying the humanity of Black people." o him, this was reminiscent of a delusion. "No matter what you tell a person who is delusional—that their belief system makes no sense and is irrational—they still feel that Black people are inferior no matter what you show them," he said. "That's a delusion. That's a fixed belief system." Poussaint has always made a distinction between everyday racism and extreme racism, the latter of which he thinks should be classified as a mental disorder. "Extreme racism is when someone gets genocidal and wants to kill. That's beyond being normal," he said. "Some of the people who object to it being called a mental disorder say, 'Well, it's just learned behavior.' It's a learned behavior to want to exterminate people because of their skin color. Not to my way of thinking." He thinks cases like 21-year-old Dylann Roof, who killed nine people at Emanuel African Methodist Episcopal Church in Charleston, South Carolina, are in this category.

Psychiatrist Carl Bell, who died in 2019, also viewed racism as a mental illness, but more akin to a personality disorder. He thought people with narcissistic personality disorder might be more predisposed to racism than others. In 2004, he wrote that people with paranoid disorders or had trauma inflicted upon them by other groups could also have racist thoughts or behaviors that are explained by those psychological disruptions. "These are all legitimate scientific questions that we as psychiatrists should be willing to test and answer," he wrote. "They still feel that Black people are inferior no matter what you show them. That's a delusion." If racism is a mental illness, it pushes the problem onto white people, Poussaint said. It acknowledges there's something wrong in the way they're thinking and feeling and relieves Black people of the feeling that if they could act differently, then white people would stop being racist against them. "Early in my career, even in college, I felt that if I was a perfect person, I could cure white people of their racism, and that's not where it's at," Poussaint said. "It's not rational. You can't undo it by being a good person and being intelligent and dressing properly. That's such a psychological burden on black people. It's part of the notion that racism is curable in that way. You can drive yourself nuts doing that." Although the APA never added racism to the DSM, people have continued giving racism clinical-sounding names, like prejudice personality, intolerant personality disorder, and pathological bias. And Poussaint has continued to advocate for thinking about racism as a mental illness since then, despite the APA's position. "Right now, there is a normalcy to it," Poussaint said. "It's a disorder among many, many people indoctrinated with the culture of insanity of slavery and Jim Crow." He thinks classifying it as a mental illness would help to fix that. "Doing so says it's a disturbance that interferes with your well-being and is an impairment." Trying to understand racism as a mental illness goes back to the 1930s, when people tried to grapple with the extreme prejudices and behaviors of the Nazis, said James Thomas, an associate professor of sociology at the University of Mississippi and co-author of the book Are Racists Crazy? But a medical model of racism couldn't fully explain people's behaviors. When covering the trials of the Nazis, Hannah Arendt wrote in The New Yorker about Adolf Eichmann, one of the top officials responsible for the concentration camps during the Holocaust. Arendt was unsettled to find that "half a dozen psychiatrists had certified Eichmann as 'normal,'" she wrote. "'More normal, at any rate, than I am after having examined him,' one of them was said to have exclaimed, while another had found that Eichmann's whole psychological outlook, including his relationship with his wife and children, his mother and father, his brothers and sisters and friends, was 'not only normal but most desirable." Sander Gilman, a professor of psychiatry at Emory University and the other co-author of Are Racists Crazy?, said that the urge to deem racism a mental illness comes from a wish to place it outside the scope of typical human behavior, when it is not. "It's a beautiful argument," he said. "I wish it were true, because what it says is that normal people like you and me should never kill people in Auschwitz. The reality is normal people regularly killed people in Auschwitz. They had so dehumanized the people they were killing that they weren't human beings anymore. That was not mental illness, that was evil because people could make choices. When we start to talk about 'normal' activity, that includes bad acts."

In other words, normal is not a synonym for "good" or "just." "I wish it were," he said. "But it's just not." Gilman said that people who have serious mental illness sometimes incorporate racist tropes into their delusions because delusions can mirror or be similar to the societies that people live in. If a person with schizophrenia disorder is treated successfully, it can help get rid of paranoid delusions, including racist ones. To Gilman, that means that schizophrenia was the underlying condition, not racism. The attempt to medicalize racism, Thomas said, can distract from the fact that racism is a systemic issue, not just an individual one. "It reflects a shift in thinking about racism as something that is interior to the self, compared to how we probably should think about racism as something that is structural and embedded." He drew an analogy to police reform in a 2016

Washington Post article. There are proposals to try and improve individual officers' prejudices through implicit bias training, for example. But this focusing on "treating" individuals ignores the larger, systemic issues that allow the police to act in racist ways overall, like "the increasing militarization of police departments, lack of oversight by law enforcement senior officials, and an approach to policing that often rewards unprovoked harassment rather than building community trust." He worries that focusing too much on the individual can ignore the context in which that person exists, which has a huge impact. When Lindsey Graham defended the choice to fly the confederate flag in South Carolina, saying "It works here," critics said that it perpetuated the extreme beliefs of white supremacists, like Roof. Graham waved this off. "It's him," he said, referring to Roof. "Not the flag." In July 2011, Anders Breivik killed 77 people in Norway by detonating a car bomb that killed eight and then shooting 69 others. When he stood for an insanity trial, psychiatrists disagreed about whether or not he had mental illness-related delusions. In a manifesto, he had written that he believed himself to be a "Knight Templar" whose mission was to cleanse Norway of immigrants. But he didn't have hallucinations or impaired cognition—symptoms of schizophrenia and related disorders. The Norwegian court decided that since his extremist beliefs were shared by other right-wing groups in Norway, they were not delusions, and they didn't let him plead insanity.

This may be one way of understanding extreme racism, as both a psychological aberration, but not an official illness—as an "extreme overvalued belief." This term is starting to be applied by some clinicians and forensic psychiatrists to extremist beliefs, like Breivik's, that are distinct from psychotic delusions or obsessions, and held by conspiracy theorists or religious cults. According to the DSM-5, delusions are "fixed, false" beliefs, which are not shared with others. An overvalued idea is different because it is shared by others in someone's culture or subculture. Unlike obsessions, another form of delusional-seeming thoughts, people don't resist or fight them off. They embrace them. These rigidly held, non-delusional beliefs "are the motive behind most acts of terrorism and mass shootings," wrote Washington University in St. Louis forensic psychiatrist Tahir Rahman in a 2018 paper. They are "often relished, amplified, and defended by the possessor of the belief," Rahman and his colleagues wrote in a paper from this year. "Over time, the belief grows more dominant, more refined, and more resistant to challenge."

Rahman compared it to acquiring a taste for food over the course of one's life. "How do you get to liking rare steak versus well done steak or medium steak?" he said. "You don't just wake up one morning and decide. These beliefs and behaviors are shaped slowly through time and through your encounters with the environment." Such beliefs can take root in anyone, not just people with mental illnesses.

"Overvalued ideas" were first described by German neurologist Carl Wernicke in 1892. But one significant change since then is the access to online information that can easily expose a person to extremist information that agrees with their belief. It's much easier now for fringe ideas to find company online, wrote Joe Pierre, a psychiatrist at the David Geffen School of Medicine at UCLA, in the Journal of the American Academy of Psychiatry and the Law.

Extreme overvalued ideas might be partially explained by cognitive distortions like "all-or-none thinking, overgeneralization, jumping to conclusions, magnification and minimization, and personalization," Pierre wrote. Other cognitive biases like confirmation bias, where people only seek out information that confirms their beliefs, and the Dunning-Kruger effect, where people are overconfident in areas where they have the least expertise, can perpetuate and strengthen false, extreme beliefs. Rahman called for more research on the non-delusional beliefs seen in cults, mass suicides, terrorism, and online radicalization, given that violence can often stem from them and that we don't yet know the best way to intervene. What is clear is that such beliefs can take root in anyone, not just people with mental illnesses. "What on the surface appears to be a mental disorder from schizophrenia to bipolar disorder may actually be a shared belief which, which anyone can develop," Rahman said. "And that is the scary part to me." The DSM has been criticized for being a collection of observed symptoms, and not effective and delineating and understanding the underlying disorders that cause those symptoms. What is the use of having such a manual, in which mental illnesses are distinguished from one another? It's so we can try to help the people with those illnesses, as crude as our diagnoses may be. Calling racism, a mental illness, and thereby treating it like one, is licensed social worker April Harter's approach. Her private practice is called the Racism Recovery Center. She said she's seen the same psychological defenses crop up in people who are racist and thinks that treating racism as narcissism and trauma can help to eradicate it.

"When you have individuals that struggle with narcissism and then they create laws and policies and educate and are in charge of school boards and they create these policies," she said, "that's what institutional racism actually is."

If people want to go to therapy for their racist attitudes, Thomas said, no one should stand in the way of them doing that. He thinks such therapy can help people think about what it means to be racist and live in a world where they benefit from privilege. "If we think that that is a policy intervention, that's where I have serious misgivings," he said. Danielle Jackson, a general psychiatry, and behavioral health resident at Yale University specializing in structural racism and health equity, feels the opposite. "I'm of the camp of feeling very strongly that it should not be added to the DSM," she said. "That is based on looking at the history of racism, and the effects of systemic racism that have been basically ingrained into the fabric of America since the beginning of the establishment of chattel slavery." If racism were officially designated as a mental illness, there could be other consequences too. "Could someone claim to be disabled from work because of racism and only be allowed to work in certain settings?" said Damon Tweedy, an associate professor of psychiatry at Duke University. "I don't think the system could contain a diagnosis of 'racism' in the way that its advocates would hope." Jackson said that if racism were added to the DSM, she would be concerned that people would try to use their diagnosis as a legal defense when charged with hate crimes. Already, because of racism, mental illness is more likely to be given as an explanation for violence by white people than people of color. This might mean we need to be extra careful about allowing mental illness as a defense. In 2015, researchers asked white Americans about two mass shootings: the Virginia Tech shooting, where the gunman was a South Korean immigrant, and Columbine, where the shooters were both white Americans. When asked about Columbine, the participants were more likely to attribute the shooting to mental illness. In contrast, when asked about Virginia Tech, people thought that the shooting was related to the shooter's identity. A formalized connection between racism and mental illness when convenient is easily exploited, as famous cases of celebrity's show.

In 2006, the actor Michael Richards called hecklers "n------" while performing at a West Hollywood comedy club. His publicist said in a statement that Richards would seek "psychiatric help." In June 2013, an NFL football player Riley Cooper, was caught on video saying, "I will jump that fence and fight every n----- in here, bro!" Cooper's statement promised he would seek help from "a variety of professionals." When Roseanne Barr tweeted a racist comment about Valerie Jarrett, an Obama administration advisor—leading ABC to cancel the reboot of her television show—Jimmy Kimmel also referred to Barr's mental health, writing in a tweet: "What [Roseanne] said is indefensible, but angrily attacking a woman who is obviously not well does no good for anyone. Please take a breath and remember that mental health issues are real. The Roseanne I know could probably use some compassion and help right now." I think that making racism a medical diagnosis would do nothing but provide a crutch to someone who had perpetrated a crime," Jackson said. "So that people like the former officers who murdered George Floyd or the neighborhood vigilantes that murdered Ahmaud Arbery would then be able to look for something like that as part of their defense. And that to me is sickening." Extreme racist beliefs, while confusing, upsetting, and wrong, can't be understood only as mental illness. These beliefs come from a hodgepodge of societal influences, cultural reassurances, cognitive biases, and a strong motivational desire to keep things at the status quo. There is one area, however, in which there is no debate on the relationship between racism and mental health—the detrimental health effects of racism on its victims. In a recent essay in Vogue, psychologist Samantha Rennalls wrote about how in light of the current protests, she has both been hopeful and also tired, reminded of the depth of the injustice she's faced on a daily basis. "Racial trauma," she wrote, "takes its toll on the Black body and soul." If calling racism, a mental illness was helpful, Jackson said, she would feel differently. Instead she thinks it's actively harmful and gets in the way of the anti-racism work on a societal level that needs to be done—the work that will actually benefit the people who suffer from racism. "I don't think [calling racism a mental illness] gives you access to any more tools to becoming an anti-racist," she said. "The work of being a racist, embracing anti-racism, and embracing social justice and equity for everyone in this country is hard individual work that folks have to do. But you also have to be committed to learning about the system in order to learn how to help do the system." Even Jane Elliott might agree. Despite her stance on racism as a mental illness, she was an advocate for early-intervention education on race and believed that racism was far from being "normal"—that it was, instead, taught to us throughout our lives. On the same Oprah segment that's recently gone viral, moments before her claim about mental illness, Elliott said, "I heard somebody in the break room say that racism is inbred. No, it is not. Racism is not part of the human condition. Racism is a learned response you have to be taught to be a racist you are not born racist. You are born into a racist society. And like anything else, if you can learn it, you can unlearn it."

Racism Is a Mental Health Crisis. We Need to Support Each Other – Here's How

Mental health and prejudice. It's important to understand how white supremacy has fundamentally harmed Black people's psyche. Black people face racial prejudice no matter where in the world they are. As a Black person, hypervigilance is always on your mind – a symptom of post-traumatic stress disorder that goes largely undiagnosed in Black people due to failures in mental health services. In the UK, Black people are more likely to suffer with severe mental health issues than any other race and are also more likely to be sectioned under the Mental Health Act. According to NHS Digital data, Black people have a detention rate of 306.8 per 100,000 in England (2018-2019) – more than four times higher than white people, where the rate is 72.9 per 100,000. Black people are also more likely to receive Community Treatment Orders – a legal order that requires a person to accept mental health treatment, including taking medication and therapy. "Racial disparity in the use of the Act is an ongoing injustice," says Vicky Nash, head of policy and campaigns at Mind. At the same time, Black and minority therapists are underrepresented in mental health services and research has shown that if a Black person's experience does not resonate with a white therapist, it can often lead to misdiagnosis. Longstanding inequalities have a weathering effect on wellbeing and mental health, which is toxic to the body's stress response system, spiking up further health issues. Black women are more prone to anxiety, depression, panic attacks and obsessive-compulsive disorders, NHS data shows.

Conditions such as diabetes and high-blood pressure are more prevalent in Black communities than any other race group and Black people are also dying disproportionately during the Covid-19 crisis, as belatedly confirmed by Public Health England. All these factors explain the vicious cycle a Black person can be stuck in traumatized by racism but facing mental health stigma; impacted by social and economic inequalities, but also by implicit biases in health care and justice.

Racism as a daily reality

As a Danish-British woman of Somali origin, and also Muslim, I've never felt like I belonged anywhere. Being a woman is difficult enough without also being a Black woman and a Muslim woman. I feel like I've always had to prove my worth in white spaces, fighting micro-aggressions like "you're so articulate," which sounds like a compliment but is actually backhanded. Are Black people not articulate? I've also suffered and continue to suffer from the 'superwoman syndrome' – not realizing this persona is a means of survival linked to a wider socio-historical context in which Black women could never display signs of weakness. This has contributed to my stress and anxiety levels, trying to be as 'perfect' as possible just to prove that I am worthy – a narrative that I need to dismantle. Being a Black person is often described as being in 'fight or flight' mode, and honestly, that is the best way to explain it. Nor am I alone in how I feel. I have been collecting the voices of Black people across the UK, Europe, and the US, asking them how racism has affected their mental health and wellbeing. "I'm tired and drained, constantly having to provide for myself in an industry and in a company among very few Black people and a sea of white faces," said one 25-year-old PR executive from London. "It's tiring to put up a front every day and dismiss micro-aggressive comments, to always be smiling and just get on with it during a fight for freedom. No one understands, they don't understand."

"The looks, the stares, the judgement and the questions alienate you from your inner being." Racism in the workplace ranges from the discreet to the blatant, a 24-year-old woman who works in marketing told me. "The looks, the stares, the judgement and the questions alienate you from your inner being. I found myself constantly adapting my language and behaviors to fit in with a group of people that wouldn't look twice at me outside of work," she says. "Being told that my natural hairstyle resembled someone that had 'put their hand in a plug socket' or seeing my non-Black friends enter high paying jobs right after graduation, while I struggled, jobless, for six months was just the beginning. Despite being told that 'by applying yourself at school and university you would achieve', being a young, Black, queer woman entails transgressing barriers that the average white woman would never have to consider." A 32-year-old teacher from New York summed it up: "I constantly have to fight and feeling like you're not heard is exhausting… it tricks you into thinking you don't matter. We are more valuable than they treat us."

This Is How to Support Black British People Right Now – And How Not To

Be Kind to Yourself

Fighting racism is not an overnight job. While we are collectively engrossed in the fight against injustice, it's important to not forget about your own personal wellbeing while supporting the cause. Look after yourself first: Talk about your feelings and offload emotional baggage. Take regular breaks from social media

Take time to reflect, meditate and journal. Keep active throughout the day and eat well. Watch light-hearted shows/movies and take your mind off the news Ask for help when you need it—vulnerability is not a weakness.

How to Support Others

As a trained Mental Health First Aider in the workplace, I recognize the impact that systemic racism can have on a person's wellbeing and the repercussions it can have if not addressed. Here is what you can do to help from today:

Listen

Actively listen to the experiences that Black people face.

Employ nonjudgmental listening skills and do not engage in racial gaslighting while doing so.

Discuss racism even if it's awkward for you. It's a privilege to learn about racism, rather than experience it on a daily basis.

Ask questions and engage in the conversation.

Most Importantly

Diversify your circle and get to know more people outside of your own race.

Reach out to a friend who you know might be affected by recent protests.

If you have Black co-workers, check in on them.

Challenge your own beliefs, prejudice, and unconscious biases.

Take charge of your own learning and be an active citizen of the world.

Continue to re-educate yourself and share your knowledge with members of your own household, family, and friends.

Use your talents, whether than be writing, speaking, filming or other creative endeavors, to raise awareness.

Finally, use your white privilege to always speak up when you witness an injustice in this world – don't be neutral.

Index

A

abolition, 4, 9
abuse, xvii–xix, 12, 36
ACA (Affordable Care Act), 43–44, 46–47, 55–56, 60–62, 64
adolescents, 29–31
  black, 29
Affordable Care Act. See ACA
Affordable Coverage for African Americans, 57
African American and Hispanic areas, 48
African Americans, 8, 11–16, 23–27, 31, 38, 43–55, 57–58, 60–62, 82
  health of, 50, 58
  impact of wealth gap on, 52
  uninsured, 46
American Psychiatric Association. See APA (American Psychiatric Association)
American Psychological Association, 11, 38
Americans, xviii, 12, 25, 44–45, 47, 64, 84
American society, 43, 47, 49
AmeriKKK, xvii, 2
APA (American Psychiatric Association), 38, 86, 88
APMS (Adult Psychiatric Morbidity Survey), 76–77
Asian British, 77
asylum seekers, 78
Auschwitz, 89

B

BAME (Black, Asian and Minority Ethnic), 4, 7, 74
  communities, 9, 74, 76, 79
  groups, 76, 79
  individuals, 75
barriers, 13–14, 27, 50, 57, 59, 75–76, 78
behaviors, 1–2, 86, 88, 91, 96
beliefs, 28, 85–86, 90–92, 94, 98
bias, 19, 50, 58
  implicit, 18–19, 96
Biden plan, 56
Black, Asian and Minority Ethnic. See BAME
Black Africans, 77
Black Americans, 7, 15–17, 19–20, 22, 80
Black and Ethnic Minority professionals, 5–6
Black British, 76
Black Caribbeans, 77
black communities, xviii–xix, 1, 8, 11, 15, 19–20, 23–24, 28, 31, 34, 79–80, 84–85, 95
Black people, xv, xviii, 5, 7, 11, 15–17, 30, 38–39, 41, 74–77, 80, 85–88, 94–98
  activists, 16
  children, 28–31
  families, xvii
  women, 41, 95–96
Black protesters, 38
Black psychiatrists, 86
Black Thrive, 79
British empire, 8
brown Americans, 7, 15–17, 19–20, 22, 80
brown communities, xviii–xix, 1, 11, 15, 20, 24, 28, 31, 34, 80, 84–85

C

celebrities, 13–14, 27, 93
　black, 13–14, 26
charities, 4, 6–7, 9, 79
children, xix, 2–3, 7, 25, 28–31, 41, 75, 89
Children's Health Insurance Program (CHIP), 55, 59
Chinese Mental Health Association, 79
chronic illnesses, 47, 49–50, 53–54
church, xvii, 20–21
compensation, 7–8
cost, 44–45, 56–57, 59
counties, 35, 53–54
Count Me In census, 76–77
country, 10–11, 33–34, 44–45, 49, 56, 80, 94
coverage, 44–46, 51, 56, 58–59
criminal justice system, 32–34, 38–39, 75
culture, 4–6, 10, 24, 74, 88, 90
　competency, 37–38
　shift, 13–14, 27

D

death, xviii, 4, 29, 31, 48, 66, 81
depressed persons, 69–73
depression, xv, xvii–xviii, 2, 12–14, 20, 27, 37, 66–68, 70–74, 78, 82, 85, 95
　untreated, 23–24
designations, 48–49
detention rates, 76–77, 95
discrimination, 8–9, 19, 58, 74, 78, 84
diseases, 11, 15–16, 50, 72
disparities, xviii–xix, 30, 38, 47, 51
DNA, xviii, 1–2
doctors, 13–14, 17–19, 27, 84, 87

DSM (*The Diagnostic and Statistical Manual of Mental Disorders*), 86–88, 92–93

E

economic indicators, 51, 53–54
education, xviii, 6, 9, 12–14, 27, 37, 47
environment, 6, 10, 25, 36–37, 91
equity, 34, 57, 94
ethnic groups, 7, 9, 44, 48, 51, 74–75, 77–78
ethnicity, 5, 18, 63, 74, 76

F

faith, xvii, 20–21
families, 12, 20–21, 45, 52–54, 59–60, 79, 83, 98
federal poverty level (FPL), 46, 49
food, 52–54, 78, 91
　insecurity, 49, 52–54
FPL. *See* federal poverty level

G

Greene King, 4–5, 8–9

H

health, xviii, 11–12, 15, 19, 33, 38, 43–44, 46–47, 49–50, 52–53, 55, 57, 59, 63, 74, 81
　equity, 57–58, 92
　insurance, 43–44, 47, 49, 56–61, 64
　services, 75–76
health care, xix, 20–22, 43–60, 64, 84, 87, 96
　premiums, 45
　professionals, 17, 19–20
　providers, 15, 48, 58
　provider shortages, 45, 48
　workforce, 59

Health Professional Shortage Areas (HPSAs), 48
Health Resources and Services Administration. See HRSA
Henson, Taraji P., 24–25
history, 3–9, 20, 24, 36, 38, 40, 80, 92
homeless, 22, 33, 49, 53–54
hospitals, 15, 17–18, 77, 87
housing, 19, 33, 36, 49, 53–54
HPSAs. See Health Professional Shortage Areas
HRSA (Health Resources and Services Administration), 48–49, 59
hunger, 53–54

I

illnesses, 34, 39, 50, 70, 86–87, 92
incarceration, 33–37, 39
inclusion, 5–7, 9
income, 43, 45–46, 52
inequalities, 3, 6, 43, 47–48, 76, 78–79, 95
inflammation, 50
injustice, 2, 6, 10, 94–95, 97–98
insurance, 3, 6, 55–58, 70
interventions, 18–19
investments, 4, 8–9

J

jails, xix, 32, 34–35, 37, 39

L

Lloyd's of London, 3–10

M

maladaptive behaviors, xviii, 1–2
mass incarceration, xix, 37, 39
Medicaid, 44–47, 49, 51, 55–56, 58–59, 61
medical care, 15, 18, 47, 53–54

medical conditions, 21, 72
medical control, 39
Medically Underserved Areas and Populations. See MUA/Ps
Medicare, 55–56, 59, 61, 64
medicine, 15–17, 19, 30, 38, 91
mental disorders, 12–14, 22, 27, 39, 66, 85–87, 92
mental health, xviii–xix, 11, 13–14, 20–21, 23–24, 26–27, 31–32, 34, 36, 39, 48, 70–71, 74–80, 82, 85, 93–96
Mental Health Act, 76, 95
mental illness, xvii–xix, 11–14, 21–22, 24–25, 27, 31–37, 39, 41, 76, 85–89, 91–94
minorities, xv, xvii–xix, 1–2, 4–5, 9–10, 15, 17–18, 20, 22, 74–75
Minority Mental Health Month, 31
MUA/Ps (Medically Underserved Areas and Populations), 49

N

Nazis, 88–89
neighborhood safety, 53–54

O

open information sessions, 13–14, 27
organizations, 4, 6–9, 26, 79
out-of-pocket costs, 45, 52, 55, 59
overrepresentation, 32–33

P

patients, 17–19, 38, 71–72, 84
people of color, xv, xvii, 32–33, 37–38, 43, 46–48, 59, 93
physicians, 15, 18–19, 84
plantations, 3, 8–9
police, 35, 38, 80–83, 90
police brutality, xviii, 80, 82
policymakers, 19, 58–59

populations, 11, 39, 43–44, 48–49, 51, 53–54, 78–79
Post Traumatic Slave Syndrome. *See* PTSS
post-traumatic stress disorder. *See* PTSD
Poussaint, Alvin, 87–88
poverty, xviii, 36, 49–51, 63, 75
prejudice, xix, 16, 19, 85–86, 90, 95, 98
prisons, 22, 34–35, 37, 39
privacy, 69
psychiatrists, 16, 88–91
psychiatry, 17, 84, 89, 91–93
PTSD (post-traumatic stress disorder), xv, 1–2, 78, 80
PTSS (Post Traumatic Slave Syndrome), xviii, 1–3
public education campaigns, 13–14, 27
public figures, 13–14, 26–27
public health, 15, 17
public option plans, 55–56

R

race, xv, xviii, 17–18, 23, 34–36, 39, 63, 76, 86, 94–95, 98
racial bias, implicit, 18
racial disparities, xviii, 17–18, 28–29, 32–33, 39, 95
racism, xix, 4, 9, 11, 17, 43–44, 48–51, 57–58, 74, 78, 80, 84–90, 92–96, 98
  institutional, 11–12, 92
  systemic, 92, 97
Racism Recovery Center, 92
racists, 4, 38, 88, 92–95
  conceptions, xv, 11
  patients, 84
  practices, 38, 53–54, 58
Rahman, Tahir, 91–92
reform, 34, 36, 45
refugees, 78

S

schizophrenia, 16, 18, 85, 89–90, 92
schools, 18–19, 25–26, 97
services, 11, 37–38, 43, 55, 76, 78
shootings, 81–83, 90, 93
slavery, 1–2, 4, 7–9, 11–12, 16, 88
slaves, 2–3, 12, 16
social factors, 44, 47, 49–51
society, 1, 3, 6, 11, 38–39, 74, 89
South, 45–47
spirituality, 20
stigmas, xv, xix, 12, 20, 25, 72, 79, 85
stress, xviii, 1, 12, 49–51, 67, 82, 96
struggles, 12, 21, 25, 27, 40, 67, 92
suicide, xix, 13–14, 23–24, 27–31, 66, 69, 77–78
survival strategies, xviii, 1–2

T

therapists, xvii, 24–26, 68, 70–71
therapy, 70, 92, 95
transient communities, 53–54
trauma, xv, xviii, 1–2, 11, 20, 24–25, 79–80, 88, 92
  childhood, xvii, xix
treatment, xv, 12–16, 18, 25, 27, 32, 35–39, 47, 50, 58, 62
trust, xix, 12–13, 15–16

V

violence, xviii–xix, 21, 23, 36–37, 85, 91, 93

W

weakness, 12, 24, 96–97
wealth, 52
wealth gap, 52
welfare, 22
wellbeing, 95–96

whites, 12, 15, 17–18, 28, 30, 40–42, 44, 47, 50–52
  children, 28–29, 48
women, 2–3, 7, 27, 35, 75, 82

Printed in the United States
By Bookmasters